"Everyone needs a moment to take a deep breath an[c] gets that. Juggling a family and being a professional 'ba[s] keeping it all pulled together, she understands a woma[n] world, cleanse her thoughts, and surrender faithfully to [C] lays out a plan, and guides the overbusy, overworked, ove[r] ...ck on track with God in the lead. This must-read book belongs with every woman regardless of age. One can never start putting priorities in order too soon. Impressive, well written, sensitive but given in tough love, Billie Jauss nails it with *Distraction Detox*." —**Cindy K. Sproles**, best-selling author of award-winning *What Momma Left Behind*

"I'm a big fan of Billie. The transparency and reality she brings to her writing is authentic and intimate. A very creative title addresses a real issue for women and men. Distractions are available to me anywhere at any time. God is not a fan. Nor am I any more. This book provides a road map to follow our way out of the messiness of distractions." —**Clint Hurdle**, former Major League Baseball player and manager

"The last couple of years have trained us to build walls from others—and even from God. Truth seems illusive, with our thoughts often scrambled and emotions unsettled and restless. Billie Jauss identifies this as spiritual jet lag, a sense that we think we're in sync with God but we're actually across the continent. In Jauss's newest book she helps the reader probe thought toxins so as to break down blockades that prevent us from freedom in our faith, bringing us to a place of confidence, peace, and personal fulfillment. I highly recommend *Distraction Detox*." —**Janet Holm McHenry**, author of 24 books, including the best-selling *PrayerWalk* and *The Complete Guide to the Prayers of Jesus*

"We live in a fast-paced world full of distractions. It can be easy for me to focus on external distractions and miss the internal work I need to prioritize to experience God's best. *Distraction Detox* is the practical and heart-changing tool I needed. In fact, I can confidently say that we all need this book as a life-changing tool. Billie's vulnerable writing style makes it feel like a trusted friend is holding your hand and heart as you examine what is keeping your heart from God's best. As a counselor I would recommend this book to all of my clients. Each chapter is the perfect balance of story to draw you in, God's word to connect your heart to scripture, and questions and actions to practically detox from your distractions." —**Jennifer Hand**, author of *My Yes Is on the Table* and host of *Coming Alive Conversations*

"Billie Jauss deftly and gently takes readers on a journey. Through the generous sharing of her own life's events, she shows us how God can break our 'unnecessary water jars'—our self-recrimination, limiting beliefs, and emotional barriers—and transform us into vessels filled with faith, hope, and purpose. Joy." —**Robin W. Pearson**, Christy Award–winning author of *A Long Time Comin'*

"Billie Jauss is an exceptional writer, and *Distraction Detox* is phenomenal. We've all been caught up in this race of life, and the curveballs thrown at us have been many. Here,

Billie shows us the importance to step back and breathe. And she does it beautifully."
—**Jason Romano**, author of *Live to Forgive* and host of *Sports Spectrum* podcast

"As a recovering people pleaser, I find *Distraction Detox* to be a powerful look at the deceptive thoughts and feelings that plague so many of us. Billie Jauss provides real-life experience and transformative scriptures that can take those who are 'stuck' into the realm of freedom. An amazing, life-changing read!" —**Tara Johnson**, author of *Engraved on the Heart, Where Dandelions Bloom*, and *All Through the Night*

"Billie Jauss brings a fresh perspective and practical biblical guidance to help overcome the mental distractions that keep us far from God. *Distraction Detox* will help you get rid of self-limiting thoughts and find peace and purpose!" —**Jon Gordon**, best-selling author of *The Garden* and *The Energy Bus*

"If you struggle with toxic thoughts, low self-esteem, or even how to live a life in step with God, this is the book for you. Author Billie Jauss is bravely transparent as she shares her own personal journey of struggling with a life of toxic barriers. Along with biblical insight and practical application, Billie gives you the tools to begin living the life God has for you. Now is the time. Walk with Billie and allow her to lead you to a life of freedom!" —**Melinda Patrick**, host of *The Even While* podcast

"A timely reminder and guide, *Distraction Detox* urges women to eliminate the emotional toxins we carry around and discover God's best for our lives. A life focused on leaving God's fingerprints wherever we are." —**Wendi Lou Lee**, author of *A Prairie Devotional*

"What an amazing and profound book! Just as we need to rid our body of toxins, we must rid our mind, spirit, and emotions of those things that keep us from a deeper relationship and walk with our Father. Billie Jauss not only uses her very personal experiences to offer insight but also provides keys to eliminating those things that keep us from fulfilling God's purpose and plan for our lives. This book isn't for the faint of heart. It requires you to take a deep look in the mirror and begin to undress before God. You will feel vulnerable but if your desire is to not just talk the talk but walk it, then this book will challenge you to lay down those things that keep you entangled and hindered. This book is powerful. Allow the Holy Spirit to use this book to bring you the freedom you need and deserve!" —**Dr. Froswa' Booker-Drew**, founder and CEO of Soulstice Consultancy

Distraction Detox

RELEASE EMOTIONAL BARRIERS.
RESTRUCTURE PRIORITIES.
REALIZE GOD'S BEST.

BILLIE JAUSS

IRON
STREAM

Birmingham, Alabama

Iron Stream
An imprint of Iron Stream Media
100 Missionary Ridge
Birmingham, AL 35242
IronStreamMedia.com

Library of Congress Control Number: 2021950040

Cover design by Robert Newell, twolineSTUDIO

ISBN: 978-1-56309-499-6 (paperback)
ISBN: 978-1-56309-503-0 (ebook)

1 2 3 4 5—26 25 24 23 22
MANUFACTURED IN THE UNITED STATES OF AMERICA

Jenn Hand and Melinda Patrick,
without your prayers and encouragement,
this book wouldn't exist.
Thank you, my friends.

Contents

CHAPTER 1
Spiritual Jet Lag

My spirit felt like a rootless tree blowing in the wind, tossed one way then the next. The discouragement of trying to please others, and myself, beat me down.

When I fought with doubt, I became discouraged. When I searched for purpose in others' opinions, I was twisted in multiple directions. My body and mind needed rest. I desired calm in the chaotic life I was leading.

Rest in Him. That still small voice whispered. *Rest in Me.* One small step toward strengthening my dependence on Jesus. When we detox from mental distractions, we can overcome the emotional barriers and find peace of mind in God.

Baseball life takes my husband, David, and me to many places in just a few days. Long road trips leave me tired, lethargic, and confused. Physically, I'd be on the West Coast, but my internal clock ticked on East Coast time or vice versa.

The bump of the tires on the tarmac jolted me awake. Gravity pulled me forward as the plane slowed to a halt. I sat upright and rubbed my eyes, smearing mascara across my face. A voice boomed, "Welcome to New York City."

New York? Why am I in New York? Grabbing my water, I took a few long swallows, hoping to clear the brain fog. The extended taxi to the gate gave me time to collect my thoughts and remember this leg of a long road trip. I settled back into my seat and sighed. West Coast last night. East Coast today.

I'd chosen to follow David from one major league baseball city to another. I traveled for years with three boys when I could. When the three were grown and flown, I followed along even more.

Traveling together was time well spent, but the wear and tear on my body and unstable emotions took their toll. Jet lag was an understatement. My body existed in one place, but internally it felt thousands of miles away. I wanted to support David, experience with him what many never experience, but I never accounted for the backlash—the jet lag of life.

Everyone on the plane seemed to move at a lethargic stumble as we exited. Those inside the terminal darted here and there. Many never stopped when they bumped into the heavy backpack I carried. I wanted nothing more than to curl up in a warm bed and sleep away the hours.

The smell of coffee drew me to a long line of travelers wanting a boost of caffeine. While I waited, a slew of thoughts bombarded me. *What is wrong with me? Why doesn't David struggle with exhaustion like I do? I'm done with all of this.*

Coffee in hand, I searched for the signs guiding me to a ride into the city. Dawn was breaking through the misty morning as I exited the terminal into the outside chill. When my turn came, I entered my yellow chariot.

As we darted through traffic, I closed my eyes and immediately fell into my habit of mentally evaluating my list of to-dos. The long baseball games and longer travel days had me running behind.

My blog post, podcast, and devotions were not finished for the week. The feeling of failure and how I should do better made me feel like a disappointment to others.

Getting to the next city on the baseball schedule earlier than the team posed obstacles. My hotel room wouldn't be ready, and my body screamed for a comfortable place to lie down. I needed time to catch my breath. But I also needed Wi-Fi to get some writing done. With the city's excitement, the calm my body longed for wouldn't happen. Jet lag is real.

The new empty-nest season brought exciting job prospects and volunteering opportunities I didn't expect. It wasn't long before expectations were pushing their way into an already busy calendar. Phrases like "The world is your oyster," "You were made for such a time as this," and "Seize the day" came from well-meaning acquaintances.

I questioned myself. I wondered what I should accomplish as an author, what needed to be done, and how I could do it all in a timely fashion. Should I

- blog more,
- blog less,
- continue the podcast,
- develop a business,
- accelerate my online presence?

Even though I had already accomplished some of those tasks, I felt unsatisfied and guilty if I sat idle. When not actively undertaking something, I meandered down a path of internal criticism and judgmental complaints. My desire for perfectionism became my focus. Discouragement soon followed.

Too many voices pushed me to feel broken and empty. I tried to please others instead of doing what God called me to do. That disobedience drove me further from peace and confidence. I began to doubt my purpose.

People tend to look for bad rather than good. I can be the worst. Have you ever had a friend tell you, "I love that you have a tender spirit, but . . ."? Or has a family member said, "I'm sorry, but . . ."? Maybe the voice in your head says, "You've got this, but . . ." The *but* negates everything before.

Negativity makes us feel "not good enough," and that often causes a disconnection with the Lord. Pointing out good causes growth. Focusing on the negative keeps us stuck.

I felt I was in control—mostly. Or was I? I devised a list for each project I needed to complete, then checked off the tasks one by one. Busyness had been the culprit before, but this time my inability to control my emotions and anxieties was the problem.

I've encountered a spiritual stagnation in certain seasons of my life. Even as I continued to do a lot of good "God things," I felt separated from Jesus. Despite the trying and doing, I wondered if my existence was as good as life gets. I repeated bad habits and blamed my busy life. Social media, Netflix, and work ate away my time. For goodness' sake, I even wrote a book about making room for Jesus.

Worries stacked like LEGO bricks and fear spiraled. Peace, rest, and fulfillment were nowhere to be found. I tried, on my own, to fix things. I'd made room in my busy schedule for time with the Lord, but the external distractions, now categorized, remained the priority.

Little by little, with each obstacle, I constructed a barrier between my spirit and Jesus's glory. Each time an obstacle arose, the feelings of more confusion, chaos, and clutter drove toxic emotions to overwhelm me. Decreasing the outside stimulus made room for Jesus, but my spiritual life and growth were not where God wanted me to be. I had a spiritual jet lag.

On our journey through *Distraction Detox*, you will come across "God-limiting" language. I want to be clear that I am not saying our emotional barriers, anxieties, chaos, or clutter can ever limit God and His amazing abilities. It just can't happen. What I am saying is that those human barriers limit *us* from seeing opportunities, receiving blessings, and growing in God. The limitations are all on the human side.

The Lord says:
"These people come near to me with their mouth
　　and honor me with their lips,
　　but their hearts are far from me.
Their worship of me
　　is based on merely human rules they have been taught."
　　　　　　　　　　　　　　　　　　　　—Isaiah 29:13

Isaiah was a prophet, an anointed representative of God. Prophets spoke for God, confronting the people and their leaders with God's commands and reminding them of His promises. Some saw Isaiah's teachings as contentious and unpopular, but for many centuries he has been considered one of the greatest prophets.

Isaiah was a strong and courageous man, confident in God's Word. He preached the message of God's redemption through Christ even before Jesus came to earth. In the beginning of his ministry, Isaiah was well-liked, but as his messages grew harsher, his listeners turned away from the teachings. It was easier to do as they pleased and think there was happiness apart from God than it was to obey His commands.

Judah's people, one of the tribes of Israel, didn't follow the prophets' guidance, yet these brave servants of God continued to proclaim the truth.

Most of God's people had fallen into their previous spiritually insensitive condition. The truth wasn't part of their hearts. Instead, they adhered to a list of rules and regulations, religious rote practice, and personal longings. Human rules dictated. They went through the motions of worshipping God. Similar to today when we forget on Monday what we learned in church on Sunday.

Isaiah preached to a group who claimed to be close to God but proved disobedient. Worship became routine, not a relationship. They wanted to receive God's blessings but not live by His standards. Distracted by the things they thought satisfied them, but instead created turmoil, they limited what God could do in and through their lives. Spiritual jet lag.

Jesus highlighted this disconnect when He called out religious leaders. The Pharisees knew a lot about God, but they didn't know God. They tested Jesus with questions, trying to trick him. These leaders wanted to prove Jesus didn't belong, and they believed their knowledge eclipsed Jesus's.

In Matthew 15, they questioned Jesus about the disciples breaking tradition by eating grain without washing their hands. The issue wasn't about proper hygiene but about a legalistic and ritualistic exercise that had no basis in scripture. The Pharisees saw handwashing as a religious duty that signaled spiritual purity.

Jesus didn't let this pass. He called the Pharisees out on their traditions, quoting Isaiah 29:13. They worshipped the Lord based on the customs they had been taught, not in response to His grace.

In all, traditions aren't bad, but these rituals allowed the religious leaders to ignore God's Word. When they replaced the Scriptures with rules, they were like Isaiah's listeners: honoring God with their lips but not their hearts.

We sometimes cite scripture even when we doubt its truth. We may speak and worship but not connect with the truth. Worship means nothing when our hearts are far from God. Turning from God when obstacles arise, building walls that separate us from the One who truly cares, or speaking but not practicing faith wastes our opportunities to serve the Lord.

Trials can be a part of God's plan for our lives. Experiencing obstacles builds character, perseverance, and sensitivity toward others. It prepares us for hardships we may face later. Effectively living out the gospel reveals our growth during challenges.

Scripture encourages us to be strong in our faith as we encounter trouble. Turning to God and breaking down the barriers builds and strengthens our faith, producing peace. God's peace.

Worry, fear, and other toxic emotional barriers unsettle us. When we chase our concerns, worry becomes our crutch. We construct unnecessary barriers with each turn or shutdown, and spiritual jet lag increases.

If our confidence in God's provisions, protection, and prevention become an after-thought, then apprehension, uncertainty, and distress build blockades. Fogginess sets in, and our peace seeps out as our emotions head toward fear.

All too often, we go to church and beg God to open His arms to us, but we keep Him at arm's length. Toxic emotional barriers keep us from unearthing the truth in our hearts and drawing near to God. We yield to negative, destructive thinking.

- How can He love me?
- I've done so many things wrong.
- I'm not good enough for Jesus.
- My wrongs are bigger than His forgiveness.
- Why don't others struggle as I do?
- My life is so messed up right now.
- I can't do anything right.
- I fail so much in my life.

This kind of emotional clutter keeps us from connecting to Jesus, hearing His voice, and realizing God's best. We leave the place of peace carrying more shame than we brought. We are unable to think at God's preferred level of clarity and peace of mind. Our mind races from one thought to another in a state of mental uncertainty. We run from our toxic emotions, which build a blockade around our heart.

The heart is the core of our being, emotions, and sensibilities. It can be broken, grow weary, and be afflicted with many other discouraging conditions. However, the good news of God changes our hearts.

Distractions create an inevitable fog of uncertainty and unsettled emotions. This spiritual jet lag is a temporary condition of being spiritually unsettled while continuing to have an active faith. We speak words of encouragement from scripture but feel like God is a million miles away from us personally. This uncertainty is not caused by sin or lack of faith but by stagnation.

The symptoms of spiritual jet lag are similar to travel jet lag. We experience an unwell feeling, have trouble staying alert, and have difficulty concentrating. Our bodies occupy space, doing good God things, but we do not feel peaceful and fulfilled. We are trapped in mental and spiritual doubt. The root problem is the internal barriers that create the disorder in our hearts and bar confidence and peace of mind. Our bodies physically occupy space in worship settings, but our hearts are miles away.

Isaiah told the people they were suffering from spiritual jet lag long before airlines existed. Jesus warned the Pharisees because they assumed they were near the Lord since they followed social rules, but their hearts were not dwelling in Him. They were doing but not connecting. They chose ritual instead of real.

Spiritual jet lag leaves us with precisely what the people of Isaiah's time experienced. They turned from God and built walls. They worshipped things, pleasing other people or themselves instead of Him. They became confused and defiant when they didn't cut out the parts of their lives the Lord found disagreeable.

Spiritual jet lag jumbles our thoughts. It scrambles our wisdom and discernment. It manifests in doubt, producing more of the same. We can feel these even when seeking the Lord because of the emotional obstacles we build in response.

We lead Bible studies, serve in the community, talk with friends about Jesus, and help with our church's needs even as we feel extreme loneliness, anger, guilt, and jealousy. We are fearful about our future, our children's future, and our marriage's negative impact.

When we feel this unsettlement and cannot find our way, we find ourselves in a very lonely place. However, we are not alone. God is with us. We can surrender to God's strength and receive His forgiveness. We can accept His holy power and control.

What Small Step Does He Want Us to Take?

What are we willing to give up to draw closer to Jesus so He can heal our spiritual jet lag? Change isn't something most of us embrace easily. Transformation comes at a cost. It means releasing the emotional barriers we hold with a tight grip, letting go of the angst of restructuring, and discerning between the meaningful and the meaningless. In the end, the great reward is the realization of God's best for our lives.

What Opportunities Are We Missing?

Wisdom comes from cleaning our fogged spirits and seeking understanding and acceptance of what Jesus has done for us. With wisdom comes encouragement and contentment in God's direction and guidance. Realizing His sacrifice leads us to be wise in our eternal goal to worship and glorify Him. Prayer and praise well up within us.

Breaking walls can increase our anxiety and expose our unsettled feelings. However, when we take risks to sever the habits that are building a barricade in our spiritual connection, we create a space of genuine involvement in our spiritual growth.

Realization of what separates us from Jesus frees us to walk where He calls us. A detox of our emotional barriers is uncomfortable. I will not promise that the process will be all rainbows and sprinkles, but I will promise that the result will be well worth the work.

God will reward anyone who gives up their spiritual blockades for the kingdom. We will be rewarded with a deeper spiritual connection to Jesus, falling more in love with Him. The overabundance of God's love in us will then spill out to others. We will have confidence in our calling. We will enjoy peace of mind, body, and spirit. Fulfillment, according to God's good and perfect will.

We will walk this path together, determining why we are distracted emotionally. We will see how identifying and removing the barriers brings freedom from our toxic restraints, builds confidence, and helps us embrace peace.

It's not about calming the chaos around us but uncovering the emotional barricade that creates spiritual jet lag. Search me, Lord, and know my heart.

We cannot control the world, but once we understand the root of our distraction, we begin to grow. Decreasing our heart's human rules allows healing, advances our growth, and propels our faith into action.

I'm excited you've decided to take the next small step in your spiritual journey. A spiritual detox reverses spiritual jet lag. Each chapter in this book will help rid you of the barricades that stop you from moving forward. Through Jesus, we are overcomers.

I pray the sharing of stories, scripture, and a step-by-step distraction detox will help you break down emotional barriers, restructure priorities, and realize God's best.

At the end of each chapter, we will take steps to detox. The Detox Challenge is not a place to feel guilt or to focus on failure. It is a plan to reclaim God's best for you. Step by step, we claim confidence, peace, and fulfillment.

Detox Challenge

Prepare for the Detox

- Create a space to sit and reflect. You can choose somewhere in the living area of your home, a corner with a bean bag, or a closet where no one can find you.
- Place your Bible, a clean journal, and a fun pen near your quiet place. Some of you will not have complete quiet, but use your space to quiet your spirit.
- Bring a fluffy pillow or silky soft blanket that makes you feel safe and comfortable. Or cuddle up with little ones.

CHAPTER 2
Tethered Toxins

I approached the baseball stadium security checkpoint with much trepidation. It was getaway day, the last day of an away series, and I planned to fly back to our home city with David and the team after the game.

Bulky items filled my backpack—things I needed to get dressed for the game because the team had taken our luggage early that morning.

"You moving in?" The usual question from ballpark security.

"Moving out." My standard response.

My well-worn backpack was large, quilted, and midnight black with multiple compartments. It held the majority of my life. Because of traveling and living in different places, the backpack contained the essentials to be easily accessible. It grew heavier each trip.

Three security officers took turns riffling through the overstuffed sack. They pulled out random items, and asked me to open the containers they couldn't see through. The impatient line of fans behind me sighed in disbelief. I could hear their mumbled words of judgment, such as why did a well-dressed woman need to carry so much into the ballpark? When security finished, I hastily repacked my bag and raced to escape the looks of annoyance, stifled laughs, and judgmental shrugs.

Instinct pushed me to run away from the feelings of being overwhelmed and burdened by the fans' scrutiny. My steps quickened as I plodded through the crowded stadium. The backpack felt extra heavy. I walked through the concourse, altering my posture and redirecting my steps to dodge long lines of fans waiting for hot dogs, buttery popcorn, and refreshing drinks. The heat from the concessions permeated the walkway. Bulky bodies, clad in local team gear, hindered easy access to a clear path.

Every eye seemed fixed on me. Between the weight of the backpack and the burden of the lingering gazes, I wanted to drop the bag and run to a quiet place away from judgment.

As I stumbled through the crowd, I wasn't being weighed down by the items in my backpack as much as the racing thoughts and feelings in my spirit. I berated myself.

- What was I carrying?
- Why did I have so much stuff in my backpack?
- Why did I do this to myself every trip?

I wanted to defend myself. My soul wrestled with turmoil, not peace—all caused by the insecurity of having to carry so much. I felt a desire to run away from the unrest but couldn't get away.

I felt I needed the loaded backpack on yet another trip. What if I left something essential behind? The panicked thought that an item may be needed always led to an overstuffed bag where the zippers barely closed.

The justification for my full backpack came quickly. It was a mental list of reasons to carry so much. Then the questions. Why do I care so much about what others say at the security checkpoint? Is the problem the items in the bag or the overwhelming personal choices of what to keep and what to leave?

When our boys were in elementary school, David and I decided to homeschool them so they could travel with us. The boys' carry-on luggage contained all their textbooks, a pencil case, and schoolwork folders. Each son's backpack was a different color—one blue, one green, one red.

If we had a short wait in the terminal or a long flight, the boys could complete their lessons. They also kept a book handy in their suitcase's front pocket for pleasure reading when there was spare time. Their backpacks held toys, electronics, and an extra coat or blanket for cold planes. Their luggage and knapsacks had multiple compartments where the boys could shove stuff they wanted to bring without Mom knowing. No matter how heavy their bags were, they managed to carry or drag them on long trips. My rule was you pack it, you carry it. I had enough of my own to lug and pull.

If we stayed for more than three days in one city, the suitcases and backpacks were unpacked entirely, emptying them of both the necessities and nonessential items. Those boys could pack an awful lot of junk in those suitcases. Once we were settled in a hotel room, we took inventory of what we had and what we needed. The boys added items at each stop, so reorganizing was an act of precision and potentially superb organization. We discarded what we didn't need to carry or what I didn't think we needed to schlep. Often, however, the boys would retrieve the castaways and repack them when I wasn't watching.

Now that I traveled alone everything stayed in my bag, adding to the weight daily. I needed to empty it to assess what was inside because the bulk of the items was holding me down. Alone, not one of the objects was heavy, but added all together, their weightiness was a burden.

Just as decreasing the activities hadn't taken away the turmoil of confusion, chaos, and clutter, cleaning out the big black quilted bag wouldn't take away my anxiety. The external interruptions were only a veil over the internal emotional barricades. The burden of feelings and thoughts caused more discouragement than the sum of all the moving parts around me.

Simplifying my schedule, taking days off from socializing, and trying to control the chaos around me didn't accelerate my spiritual growth. The weight that pressed on my soul was an emotional burden, actually many burdens: discouragement, judgment, unworthiness, fear, loneliness, feeling unloved, and more.

Emotional barriers created tall walls, which led to self-limiting behaviors. Worse than hindering myself and all I could do and be, the barricades were restricting me from using my God-given gifts. Distraction filled me with a sense of failure and shame.

God-restricting actions compromise God's best for us. They stifle opportunities to connect with Jesus and other people, to live with confidence, and to embrace peace. The tethered toxins of emotional condemnation limited my ability to think, act, and be more Christlike. I avoided relationships, turned down invitations, and shut down opportunities to glorify God. All of this because my mind and spirit gathered cluttering toxins that separated me from activities and other people.

The woman said to him, "Sir, give me this water so that I won't get thirsty and have to keep coming here to draw water."

He told her, "Go, call your husband and come back."

"I have no husband," she replied.

Jesus said to her, "You are right when you say you have no husband. The fact is, you have had five husbands, and the man you now have is not your husband. What you have just said is quite true."

"Sir," the woman said, "I can see that you are a prophet. Our ancestors worshiped on this mountain, but you Jews claim that the place where we must worship is in Jerusalem."

—John 4:15–20

Jesus had conversations with many people. He spoke on a spiritual level, but they heard from an earthbound plane. He focused on their deepest needs no matter what burdens they dragged and helped them see the deeper spiritual truths. A typical conversation with Him turned into a life-changing encounter—like the day He met a Samaritan woman.

In that era, the townswomen of Samaria went to the well in the morning while the temperature was cooler. It was their job to retrieve the daily water needs while their husbands were working. The journey to the well was their gathering time, their prayer time, a time to vent and be encouraged. Together they shared on the way, picking up the latest recipe or a new sewing technique. It was their social circle.

Today, women go to the bathroom in groups when out. One woman gets up to go, and the other women tag along. As they enter the bathroom, the conversation has already progressed beyond small talk. They know exactly where to take the conversation quickly. They share personal information, encourage one another, complain about their children's behaviors—all the while standing in solidarity with one another.

In Samaria, imagine the different groups of women—older and younger, mothers, the childless, those living nearby—meeting at the corner and meandering down the road together with their water jugs in hand. Some walked quickly while others took their time. Smiling, chatting, and full of joy, they gathered to tackle the day's work together.

After they retrieved the water, the women walked back to the village to start their day and accomplish their other tasks. The support of the other women made their jugs lighter. The relationships strengthened the freedom to share and support.

But the Samaritan woman went to the well at noon, carrying her water jug and a ton of remorse, sadness, and sorrow. Hot. Weary. Alone.

She probably chose to go to the well alone at noon to avoid the women who ostracized her. She thought she would be safe.

On that day, however, someone was there. A Jewish man lounged by the well in the heat of the day. As she approached, she would have been apprehensive.

In the days of Jesus, Jews and Samaritans did not associate with one another. Additionally, women and men were not to be alone together unless they were married. There were so many reasons she would have been cautious about approaching the well, but the necessity for water outweighed her wariness.

Many preach about this woman being a sin-filled person. They create stories about why she would have had five husbands. The wayward woman Jesus talked to at the well has been called a prostitute and a divorcée. She's been labeled promiscuous, an overall terrible, immoral person.

Yet Jesus was there waiting for her.

Many sermons and opinions declare she divorced her husbands. But at that time, women had no legal rights to end a marriage. Could there be another reason?

I challenge you to look at her in a different light. Nothing in the Bible says that any of her marriages ended in divorce, nor does it state she had lived with the first four men without being married. Let's look at her with a what-if perspective:

- What if she wasn't divorced?
- What if her five husbands died?
- What if the man she was with was the brother of the five men who had died?
- Would he want to marry her even if those were the standards of the time?
- What if the five men abandoned her and married other women?
- What if none of this was her fault?
- What if the village shunned her because all five husbands left her?
- What if she was seen as cursed because five men who married her died or left?

Jesus brought up the reason she was there alone: the number of husbands. He didn't give the reason she had five husbands, just the fact. Jesus wasn't judgmental or accusatory. He stated fact.

"I have no husband." Shame dripped from her soul. I envision her head bowed as she admitted the weight of her confession. Could she have been thinking, *Is this as good as it gets?* Jesus brought her past to the surface. The feelings that simmered in her soul probably accelerated to a rapid boil. Maybe she wanted to run away from her uncomfortableness, but something about Jesus captivated her.

The burden of knowing she was an outcast likely weighed heavy in her spirit and mind. She would have known what the women were saying. She would have created stories of what they were thinking. If her husbands abandoned her, no woman would want to go near her because their husbands may do the same thing. What if her stigma followed them home? She must be cursed if she had five dead husbands. What woman would want to endanger her own marriage? Who would want to risk their lives?

Whatever the reason, the other women did not include her. They distanced themselves from her, and she distanced herself from them. The weight of their words. The burden of past experiences. The heaviness of feeling the feels, fear, loneliness, and shame—all inhibited her opportunities for encounters, relationships, and support.

The Samaritan woman's story had taken on a life of its own, and she became lost in the drama. Relationships were compromised. The townswomen had ostracized her from their social group—the emotional distractions dragged her further into isolation. Walls were erected. People avoided her.

She was no longer married. She was living with a man who wouldn't or couldn't marry her. She went on with her mundane life and carried the judgment of others and herself—the emotional toxins.

The Samaritan woman was stuck where she and others had placed her. She was frozen in the quagmire of loneliness, cemented inside the brick walls of judgment. A well of emptiness restricted her from being the woman God created her to be. It inhibited her beliefs and labeled her with wrong characterizations.

When Jesus spoke of her husbands, the Samaritan woman changed the subject. She thought she could distract Jesus and His discussion of discouraging issues. But He redirected her self-limiting beliefs from what she couldn't, wouldn't, or shouldn't do to what He could do in and through her life. He challenged her to recognize her self-imposed limitations.

Jesus explained His living water. She didn't see the spiritual value at first, only the practical value of ease and comfort. She wouldn't have to come to the well each day to retrieve water. She wouldn't have to go to the well alone, secluded from other women. She wanted the easy way out.

She confessed that she knew the Messiah was coming.

Jesus responded, saying, "I am He."

Imagine the weight of those words, the light-bulb moment when she first believed.

When the disciples returned to Jesus at the well, they were shocked that He was talking with the woman. She quietly distanced herself from them, then left her water jar—her sole source of water—and returned to the town. She also left behind the emotional burdens carried in her spirit.

After talking with Jesus and believing He was the Messiah, the Samaritan woman left the vessel carrying what she *thought* was essential to life and ran back to the village to tell others what *is* essential to life. She acknowledged God's best. She released the emotional barriers and shared her experience with the townspeople.

The scorned Samaritan woman abandoned her water jar and her limitations. She told everyone about her encounter with Jesus. Joy burst forth. The townspeople listened and believed her. They then discarded their opinions of her past and made their way toward Jesus and the future.

Because the woman shared her story, she let go of her limiting beliefs. She shared her God story. And many believed.

Each of us carries a backpack of mental, emotional, and spiritual clutter—emotional toxins like fear, loneliness, and anger. Even unforgiveness, shame, and decreased worth linger just below the surface and cause self-limiting beliefs that restrict God's best for us. These tethered toxins are our unnecessary water jars.

There will always be circumstances in our lives we cannot stop. Life happens around us. We can simplify the external distractions and the world's chaos, but not all of it. Every day, things happen that we don't expect or plan. We all have tethered toxins that need to be exposed. We have no easy way out. The hard work needs to be done, and we have to leave the nonessential things behind.

Our emotional reaction to external stimuli builds the walls of self-protection, self-deprecation, and self-limitation. Toxic thoughts or actions can lessen our belief in what God can do in and through us. His best.

But we don't have to carry the heaviness. All the self-limiting beliefs, shame, pain, and burdens need to be left behind at the feet of Jesus.

Our life is full of items we need to focus on during different seasons. There's no need to fixate on the feelings of what others place on us—or what we place on ourselves—that restrain us from being who God has created us to be and do. The toxins infiltrating our spirit will outweigh the more profound qualities and gifts God gives us.

My backpack and its contents were not the problem when I walked into that ballpark on getaway day. Nor was the act of getting water alone or carrying the water jug the issue for the Samaritan woman.

Complications arose when I gave free rein to thoughts of others' judgment, condemnation, assumptions, and accusations. Those thoughts opened a floodgate of past experiences, current struggles, and future projections of pain.

We aren't always physically carrying items that weigh us down, but we often lug around pounds of emotional barricades that poison our spirit rather than protect us. Guilt, shame, and regret are tethered to us like cement blocks in our spirits.

What are you carrying?

Identifying these tethered toxins starts the distraction detox. Releasing the discouragement and opening up to more confidence and peace brings about transformation.

When my kids returned to public schools, one of the things we disliked the most was cleaning out their backpacks at the end of the school year. Dumping the contents on the floor was the first step in cleaning them out. Spraying with disinfectant came next.

The rank smell, the junk accumulated at the bottom, the unneeded items, and the dirt. At first, the stuff looked like a pile of garbage. Searching through the assortment of articles, we sometimes found a gem—or a dirty gym sock. One by one, we evaluated the worth or burden of each item.

The gems—a heart-shaped rock found in a parking lot, a baseball card signed by their favorite player, or a piece of notebook paper with the lineup—were brushed off, read, and kept. The grimy gym sock got the boot straight to the trashcan because there is no saving anything so putrid.

We do the same with our backpacks of tethered toxins—dump, reveal, toss, keep. We evaluate the worth or burden of each item and its effect on our spiritual health.

- Shame taints courage.
- Lonesomeness hinders connection.
- Fear stops bravery.
- Discouragement poisons authentic relationships.
- Our feelings of unworthiness limit God's power to work in us.

Our initial step to the distraction detox begins when we recognize and acknowledge the unwanted, unnecessary emotional distractions in seasons of discouragement and defeat. Detoxes are cleansing. Cleansing releases us from the tethered toxins.

What do you need to leave behind—guilt, shame, regret?

Are there self-limiting beliefs holding you back from opportunities to glorify God?

Are there God-limiting actions creating a stagnant spirit?

Are you settling for the unimportant?

Detox Challenge

Go to your room!

(Your prayer room, quiet place, or designated seat)

- Always begin with prayer. Invite Jesus in.
- Close your eyes.
- Take three deep breaths through your nose. Blow out from your mouth with force.
- Reflect on a time when a significant burden held you back from God's best.
- Ask God to reveal any compromising situation He wants you to recognize.
- What do you see, feel, hear?
- Acknowledge a self-limiting action, speak it out loud, then write it down.
- Acknowledge God-limiting actions where you are settling for the unimportant. Speak them out loud. Write them down.
- Ask God to forgive you for limiting opportunities during the compromising situation and for the barriers you erected since.
- Write a prayer of thanksgiving for what you expect God to do through this detox process. His detox process.

CHAPTER 3
Reality in Truth

The flight attendant's announcement was light and cheery. My heart was heavy and sad. A few hours earlier, my phone had rung. "Are you awake?" my sister asked. It was 2:33 a.m. David and I had gone to bed only an hour before. Was she so excited I was visiting in a couple of days that she couldn't wait to talk?

I confirmed I was awake but hazy. Then I heard the terror in her voice. The call no one ever wants to get, no one wants to believe.

David and I were up late the previous night packing for a two-week vacation to my hometown to see my family. I hadn't seen my mother in six months. The pandemic was raging, but we felt safe taking an RV trip north—our first summer getaway in thirty years. COVID-19 had canceled the baseball season, and David was working from home. All we needed was electricity, the internet, and a safe way to travel.

Two weeks earlier when we discussed the trip, I said, "This year can't get any worse, so let's go." *Worse* wasn't the right word for what I heard coming from the other end of the phone.

I am the baby of eight kids. My father had four kids in his previous marriage. My mother had three. Together they had me.

The sister on the phone was the second child, the oldest girl of my mother's children. She lived with my mother and our oldest brother. My second thought was something had happened to them. My mind ran wild as my sister tried to talk through her tears.

She went on to tell me that the house our sister Helen and her husband, Larry, lived in was on fire. Their twenty-nine-year-old son had gotten out, but they did not.

This couldn't be true.

"You're lying!" I said.

"They didn't get out!" she screamed.

There was no way this was happening. I curled up on the cold leather couch and began to shiver.

"You know Larry," I said. "He's on a tractor, pulling stuff away from the house. Find him, and you'll find Helen."

I couldn't accept the truth.

Other family members arrived at her house as we ended our call.

I sat up, hands on my knees, and cried out to Jesus. David came to my side. Tears didn't come just yet. I still needed verification it was true.

Within thirty minutes, the news was confirmed. Helen and Larry had not gotten out. Again, I cried out to Jesus. "Lord, accept them with open arms. Let them know how much You love them."

I was on a plane four hours later. The flight attendant chirped out instructions over the intercom as my thoughts raced. My heartbeat was harder, faster, and louder than the engines as we took off.

Why?

How can this be?

What about Mama?

Will she survive losing them?

What will Helen's boys do?

How could this happen?

I can't imagine our family without them.

Why me, Lord? Why them?

How can something like this happen?

Not our family!

My thoughts turned inward. Regret filled me. Why hadn't I called the previous weekend when I felt the urge to pick up the phone? What are we going to do as a family? Did they know how much I loved them?

I closed my eyes, trying to rest, but memories flooded my mind like the pictures in my social media memories. I could see their silhouetted outlines in the darkness. Hear their laughter. There was no chance of sleep with my thoughts darting directionless.

The plane gained altitude, but the peace that my faith normally provided was left behind on the tarmac. Turmoil gained momentum in my spirit, climbing as the plane leveled off.

How absolutely lovely my sister was. My brother-in-law's wide, mischievous grin. The fights we had. The hugs we gave. Words that were said. The words left unsaid.

My heart felt like it would explode. My head pounded, and hot tears trickled down my cheeks onto my mask.

Leaving so early in the morning, I had spoken to only one of my boys. I knew the other two were still sleeping at that hour. Tension rose in me as I landed in my connection city. I knew more challenging conversations lay ahead. That kind of news is not easy to hear and harder to say.

Clarity was fleeting. The unreal feeling. I felt like I was watching a television show being filmed. I wasn't involved, yet I was walking on set. Slowly. In a fog.

Unsteady. Lightheaded.

Sorrowful. Weepy. Frustrated.

The roller coaster of emotions battled with denial, reasoning, and anger.

When I landed, I called David. His support was always steady and affirming. I still felt the hugs he'd given me before I left. He knows how I let my thoughts get away from me, so he prayed before leaving me at the airport, asking Jesus to give me a clear mind, a peaceful soul, and a way to shine Christ through the tragedy.

But I had left his prayer in the car and carried the torment into the terminal. Hearing his voice again as I began my drive, the seed of his prayer began to take hold. He had spoken to our youngest but our oldest still didn't know.

There's no easy way to share the news of a family tragedy. I was overwhelmed with dread each time I clicked on a son's name in my Favorites list. I couldn't protect their hearts. We cried. We comforted one another with loving words. I was trying to hold it together as much as possible. Inwardly, where no one could see, the trouble raged.

The last call before my flight home was to my mother. My eldest niece had given her the news. Mama yelled and screamed. Grief suffocated her, tears flooded. She accused my family of lying and being cruel. Denial is very real.

Her first words to me were, "You have to get home. What are we going to do?" She repeated that question numerous times over the next week. Each time I answered, "I don't know what we're going to do, but we'll do it together." My love-laced words held more strength than my broken heart.

The next flight, the final leg of my trip home, was the longest. I was ready to arrive physically, but mentally, I didn't want to land. After I got my rental car, I had an hour's drive until I faced reality.

I could have kept my thoughts pure and right, but I chose the torture myself. I ruminated over the unforgiveness between my sister Helen and me.

- What did I say last?
- Was she still mad at me from that argument we had years ago?
- Did the hurt tear at our relationship more than I knew?
- Did she know how much I loved her?

Regret raged. Things said. Things unsaid. No last hug. No last "I love you."

Remorse. Sorrow. Guilt.

Fear filled me. Fear of what I would see, what I would say, how the family would feel and react.

Pain and sorrow overcame me with each mile.

I approached the exit to Helen's house but couldn't drive down the ramp. Pulling to the side of the road, I collapsed on the steering wheel.

A day without sleep.

A spirit without hope.

Anger. Doubt. Regret. Pain.

Overwhelming pain.

My mind wandered in many directions, none of which were good and righteous.

I have no peace, no quietness; I have no rest, but only turmoil.

—Job 3:26

I avoided the book of Job for years. I had only heard the negative details of how God allowed Satan to attack Job even though he was a righteous man. I'm sure other things were taught in sermons, but I tend to get caught in the negative.

In the months after our family's tragedy, I begged God to send me to a book that would help me. He gave me the book of Job. I didn't want Job. But, Job was exactly what I needed.

After reading the entire book, I realized tragedy wasn't the theme. The book of Job demonstrates God's sovereignty and the meaning of true faith. It answers the question, Why do the righteous suffer?

Job was a prosperous farmer who owned thousands of animals. He had ten children and many servants. He was a righteous man, a model of trust and obedience to God. A priest.

Let's just say Job wasn't the kind of person who acted one way at church and another way in the marketplace. He feared God and took Him seriously. Job lived his life to honor God.

Four back-to-back calamities happened—all at the hand of Satan and all allowed by God. Hard to hear, but Satan asked God and God said yes. God's goal was to purify and sanctify Job, not to take him out.

Job lost everything: his children, his livestock, his servants, and even his physical health.

After the tragedies and physical attacks, Job cursed the day of his birth. Distress and disappointment led him to believe he would never have happiness again. He complained and questioned God. He felt far from the Lord but never denied Him.

In his pain, he was discerning the truth—what he knew about God versus the deception of what Satan wanted him to believe.

Job let his mind wander, piling up a stack of barriers that led him to misery and anguish.

"Why, God? Why are you doing this to me? I've done nothing wrong." Some of the same questions and comments I've hurled at God in times of trouble.

That day on the way to my sister's house, I sat in the rental car on the side of the road asking questions maybe I shouldn't. My soul cried out in anguish: "Why? Why? Why? Lord, I've loved you with my whole heart. How can this be? How can this happen? Why is our family your target?"

Job's wife told him to curse God and die, but Job suffered in silence. (I'm no expert, but my suggestion is don't be that wife!) He chose to believe in the goodness of God. He asked his wife, "Should we accept good from God and not trouble?" (Job 2:10).

He was such a wise man.

The questions toward God came easy to Job. Brick by brick, he erected a wall of doubt, defense, and disappointment. He never questioned God's sovereignty, but he did doubt God's love for him. Isn't that what Satan wants? Lies plastered over our spiritual eyes so we can't see God's hand in the struggles.

Job experienced extreme physical pain as well as grief over the loss of his family and possessions. His grief placed him at the crossroads of his faith. His thoughts created barriers in his heart, and he believed God was no longer his protector.

He had lived a life being careful not to worship material possessions or status; he worshipped God alone. But he was overwhelmed by calamities that mocked his caution and left him confused and uncertain as to why these tragedies would be happening despite his right living. The foundational principles of his life seemed to crumble. Job lost perspective. He built a fortress forty stories high when he verbalized his arguments and questions.

Job felt alone. He wrapped himself in thoughts of death. He felt far from God and continued to ask why. Job defended God one minute and doubted the next. I'm thankful I'm not alone in the confusion of defending and doubt.

In comes Elihu, the youngest of Job's acquaintances, who rebuked the other friends for their inability to give Job a reasonable answer for his suffering. Elihu's partial answer was people cannot understand all that God allows; instead, they must trust Him.

The young man was long-winded, but Job needed to hear what he said. Elihu helped Job see that his desire to understand why he suffered overwhelmed him and made him question God. The anguish and distress kept him from seeing the goodness of God.

Elihu concluded his speech with the tremendous truth that faith in God is far more important than an explanation for suffering. He pointed Job back to the Lord. God was not done with Job.

Are we taking our minds down a winding path of condemnation, anger, or anguish? Are we making more trouble in our minds by adding anxiety, chaos, and turmoil rather than allowing ourselves comfort in Jesus?

Most people say transformation begins in the heart. When our hearts are at peace, we can trust in the Lord and His plan. Let's look at transforming the mind. We cannot grow our spiritual hearts if our thoughts are out of control.

If we focus on what's wrong—reviving hurts and pain, restoring regret, strengthening shame, or feeding fear—we live with emotional barriers that keep us from understanding what's right and true.

A Harvard research psychologist's study revealed mind-wandering is often the hidden source of distraction. "A human mind is a wandering mind, and a wandering mind is an unhappy mind. . . . The ability to think about what is not happening is a cognitive achievement that comes at an emotional cost."[1]

Brain science reinforces the need to manage our minds. "Mind management has become more important than time management." We cannot control all our thoughts, but we can test them as they come. Truth or deception? I believe the "beginning of everlasting transformation and sustainable growth" begins in the brain.[2]

What if we could remove the barriers causing spiritual jet lag by managing our minds? I know we can.

Because Job did not capture and control his thoughts at the beginning of his tragedies, his troubles tormented him more. When God finally spoke to Job and his friends, Job stopped his chaotic thoughts.

Out of a mighty storm, the hurricane of twisting thoughts, the drenching rain of tormenting words, and the raging noise that had built within Job—God began to ask questions. He used Job's ignorance of the earth's natural order to reveal his ignorance of God's moral order. If Job did not understand the workings of God's physical creation, how could he possibly understand God's mind and character? There is no standard higher than God Himself. God is the standard by which everything is measured. He alone established His authority.

Where was Job when all of creation was done? Who was he to question God's infinite wisdom? God laid the foundation of the faith Job once trusted. He put Job's thoughts back into line one at a time. God proved His supremacy.

The Father was not seeking answers from Job; He was leading him to recognize and submit to His authority. Only when Job stopped and quieted his thoughts was he able to hear what God said. Job then admitted,

---

[1] Steve Bradt, "Wandering Mind Not a Happy Mind," *The Harvard Gazette,* November 11, 2010, https://news.harvard.edu/gazette/story/2010/11/wandering-mind-not-a-happy-mind/.
[2] "You Are What You Think About," The Daily Coach, October 18, 2019, https://thedailycoach.substack.com/p/you-are-what-you-think-about.

I am unworthy—how can I reply to you?
    I put my hand over my mouth.
I spoke once, but I have no answer—
    twice, but I will say no more." (Job 40:4–5)

Job's mind was captivated by the knowledge and wisdom of God. Being a believer doesn't mean we don't have times of doubt. God can handle our doubts and will deal with them as long as we keep communication open. Pray. Keep listening to Him.

God welcomes our sincere questions with loving answers. If we don't think deeply about Him, we can't know Him deeply. Doubts and questions are part of that process. He gladly answers them in the Scriptures and when we are in prayer, crying out to Him.

God also admonished Job's friends. He condemned them for speaking to Job as they did. They were not speaking truth, as Job spoke of God's righteousness.

Pulling to the side of the road before exiting toward my sister's house, I begged God for His Holy Spirit and His guidance.

Oh, dear Jesus. Go before me. Give them the peace that only you can give. Lord, help me to gain control of my mind. Fill me with your Holy Spirit so that I am a vessel of your love and kindness. Take away this torment. Give me clarity. Keep my soul safe from the Enemy's torture. Lord, I need you. Oh, how I need you. I can't do this alone. I can't do this at all. Only You can. Fill me with your Holy Spirit. Tame my thoughts. Help me focus.

In that instant, I felt the Lord's peace, as He brought order to my heart, soul, and mind. I heard His voice in my soul: *One thing at a time. One thought at a time.*

One thought at a time. Renewing our minds leads to everlasting transformation and sustainable growth in Christ. When we change our thinking, we begin to flourish in every area of life. Discerning each thought—truth or deception?—reveals the lies Satan uses to keep us trapped.

We have a relationship with Christ, but we also have a relationship with our thoughts. A wandering mind limits what God can do in and through us.

Capturing obstructive thoughts as they needle their way into our soul and erect walls is the beginning of purposeful change. Managing our mind is an integral part of the distraction detox.

Sometimes our wandering mind takes us to a place of false security. When we meander down a road of anxiety and stress, we take that thought captive and head in a more comfortable direction. Even when we are going in a safe direction, we have to question if the new idea is truth or deception. It may be more comfortable than the last, but is it safe?

As we renew our minds, the Holy Spirit will remove false beliefs and unhealthy thought patterns and redirect us to His good, pleasing, and perfect will for our lives. With God's guidance, we can learn to conquer mental clutter.

Our relationship with Jesus and our mind will profoundly influence our lives, parenting, career, leadership, and relationships. The most significant limits we have are the ones we impose on ourselves. As we detox our minds from emotional barriers, we move from mind wandering to freedom and purpose. It's not an easy process, but it is totally worth it in strengthening your spiritual growth.

One practice I use to overcome mind-wandering is mind management or mindfulness. The definition of mindfulness is "the practice of maintaining a nonjudgmental state of heightened or complete awareness of one's thoughts, emotions, or experiences on a moment-to-moment basis" (*Merriam-Webster*).

Mindfulness is to be fully present and attend to what is happening now—focusing on each thought. Being fully present in the presence of Jesus.

God meets us when we cry out to Him.

Detox Challenge

- Always begin with prayer.
- Pay attention to your thoughts. Increase your awareness of the thoughts that hold you back.
- Activate your trust in what the Lord can and will do in and through your detox.
- Accept responsibility for your thoughts.
- Take one thought and hold it for a while. How many times do you have that one thought?
- Is that thought truth or deception?
- Show yourself some grace. Jesus gives grace on grace.
- What helps you manage your thoughts—a trusted friend, God's Word, a sermon or podcast?
- What doesn't help? What allows negative thoughts to gain momentum and seem uncontrollable?
- Continue to take each thought captive. Write it down. Keep a running list of those thoughts during the day.
- We will work on replacing those thoughts in chapter 4.

CHAPTER 4
Take Off the Grave Clothes

Do I have a sign on my head that says, "Tell me anything you want, even if it hurts me?" My entire life, people have assumed I can handle anything they say to me. I exude confidence and strength on the outside, so maybe others feel they need to take me down a notch.

Have you ever had people say things like:

- I can't believe you are wearing that.
- Nothing was the same after you were born.
- How did you write a book?
- God can't love a girl like you.
- Nobody can love someone like you.
- Your sin list must be very long.
- What makes you think you can be my friend?
- You're the lead in the show. That's surprising.
- He'll marry you, but he won't stay.
- You'll never be a good mother.
- Your children will walk away and never speak to you again once they have a choice.
- Your husband must cheat on you.
- Your mother had a better life before kids.

When people say things that cut deep into my soul, they may think they're being funny, bringing me back to their reality, or stating the obvious. But their comments unearth the self-limiting beliefs I already hold in a mental storage chest. I pull them out one by one, searching for proof the statements or questions are correct.

How many times do we allow words to root themselves in our spirit, creating beliefs and self-limiting behavior that result in God-restricting actions?

After thirty-three years involved in professional baseball and eighteen in the major leagues, I still don't feel like I belong in the major league wives' section. I've struggled with my value in relation to my husband's job. Others have told me I don't belong.

One experience was horrible, which is not the norm with the wives. When David took a position with a new team, one of the wives decided she didn't understand why my husband got a coaching position. She had no clue he had been in the big leagues for many years before this position. She focused on the fact that he'd never played professional baseball.

Every time she saw me—yes, every game—she asked me how he got a big-league job. She thought no man should be allowed to coach in the major leagues if he hadn't played professionally. David worked hard for many years to overcome the stigma, but this wife felt it was her duty to put me in my place and make sure everyone else knew.

I fought the feeling that the other wives felt the same way. My lack of self-value exploded. Personal insecurities made me think I didn't belong. My desire to disappear from the group prompted me to shut down. I wrapped myself in the statements this woman spewed at me, wore them as truth, and distanced myself from the other women.

As the other wives saw her behavior, they were intentional to include me. It took me a bit longer to trust their intentions and desire to accept me for who I was, even if David hadn't played professionally.

Over the years, I also grappled with giving up my career to support David. From childhood, I wanted to be a nurse. I began volunteering at the local hospital when I was eleven years old. Within the year, I secured a volunteer spot in the emergency room every Friday night from 7 p.m. to 11 p.m. The day I turned sixteen, I started my first paying job at a nursing home.

After high school, I went to Atlantic Christian College in Wilson, North Carolina, and majored in nursing. The competition was intense since lots of others had the same dream.

While there, I met David. We moved to Florida, and I entered Florida Atlantic University to finish my bachelor's degree in nursing. Upon graduation, I earned a spot in an internship program to ensure a job in an intensive care unit (ICU).

When I began my career in the ICU, some of the more experienced nurses didn't agree with the policy of new graduates working in the unit. They ostracized the women and men who entered without years of experience on the regular floors in the hospital.

I was qualified to be a nurse. I had the degree, the experience, and the critical care training that proved my value. But I struggled with feelings of inadequacy when having to implement knowledge from the classroom. The internal struggles made me cower on the inside and question my professional abilities.

As with many life experiences, the avalanche of thoughts swept from one extreme to another, stopping in places like:

- I'm not good enough.
- I'm a failure.
- I don't belong.
- They are going to realize I'm not that good.
- Someone is going to tell me I am in the wrong place.
- I have no place here.
- I'm not that smart.

Some of these thoughts were the opinions of others, but most were self-imposed from years of feeling like a fraud. Other people's words cut deep, but the words I spoke to myself were, and are, the biggest bullies of all.

Self-limiting beliefs stem from our thoughts and hold us back from all God desires to do in and through our lives. These thoughts impose a feeling that we do not belong to our community or that our accomplishments are illegitimate, a demeaning, self-imposed perception.

A study by Pauline Rose Clance and Suzanne Imes in 1978 at Georgia State University indicated that high-achieving women often suffered from imposter phenomenon. The term is "used to designate an internal experience of intellectual phoniness that appears to be particularly prevalent and intense among a select sample of high achieving women."[3]

I haven't done an extensive study of women. However, living in the baseball world for over thirty years, I've been in contact with many different wives and girlfriends. During deep conversations over the years, I've found we all have self-limiting beliefs that freeze us in a place of defeat and discouragement. We feel like phonies. We fear we will be found out and reveal we don't belong, so we cover our true self with who we think we should be and limit our ability to overcome discouragement.

In whatever season of life, women feel inadequate where they are and with what they are doing. As I captured each thought, I revisited many stages of my life and the beliefs that lingered from each.

My school days were hard because I didn't believe my efforts were enough to keep up with the smarter kids, even though my grades were good. *I'm not smart enough.*

When I was given the lead role in *Alice in Wonderland* with my ballet school, I was so nervous the directors would realize they made the wrong decision and take it away from me that I turned it down. *Someone is going to show up and tell me I'm in the wrong place.*

Trying out for the high school cheerleading squad, I kept waiting for someone to confirm I wasn't good enough, even when I was chosen for the front line. *I'm not good enough.*

I was so excited when the pregnancy test was positive with our first child. Then the thoughts of possibly being a bad mom terrified me. *I will fail.*

---

[3] Pauline Rose Clance and Suzanne Ament Imes, "The Imposter Phenomenon in High Achieving Women: Dynamics and Therapeutic Intervention," *Psychotherapy: Theory, Research & Practice 15*, no. 3 (1978): 241–47, https://doi.org/10.1037/h0086006.

Recurring thoughts are a hard habit to break. But mind management helped me see I couldn't clear all the racing emotions on my own. These examples of self-limiting beliefs that lead to God-restricting actions need to be identified.

What if we could remove the barriers that cause spiritual jet lag by naming the deceptive thoughts and countering them with the truth? I know we can.

Self-limiting beliefs hinder our ability to overcome the raging thoughts and hurtful memories. We cannot stop damaging comments from others, but we can choose what builds a home in our mind and heart.

Choosing to replace deceptive thoughts with truth is a commitment. God has called us into His marvelous light. Commit to moving forward. Come out of darkness and into the light.

When he had said this, Jesus called in a loud voice, "Lazarus, come out!" The dead man came out, his hands and feet wrapped with strips of linen and a cloth around his face. Jesus said to them, "Take off the grave clothes and let him go."
—John 11:43–44

In John 11, Jesus's friend Lazarus was sick. His sisters, Mary and Martha, sent word to Jesus. Jesus loved Martha, Mary, and Lazarus, but Jesus lingered where He was. He said, "This sickness will not end in death. No, it is for God's glory so that God's Son may be glorified through it" (John 11:4).

Two days later, Jesus was ready to go back to Judea. The disciples warned Him of the threat of stoning Jesus had spoken of earlier. He told them to walk by daylight when they could see, for a person who walks at night stumbles because they have no light.

When Jesus arrived in Bethany, Lazarus had been in the tomb for four days. Martha confronted Jesus as He entered the village. She wasn't kind in saying her brother wouldn't be dead if Jesus had come earlier. She blamed Him, but she hadn't lost hope.

Jesus told her He had power over life and death as well as the power to forgive sins. Whoever believes in Christ has a spiritual life, even death cannot conquer or diminish in any way.

Even though Martha had been too busy to sit and talk with Jesus when He visited her home on a previous trip, she was a woman of deep faith. "Yes, Lord," she replied, "I believe that you are the Messiah, the son of God who is to come into the world" (John 11:27).

Martha returned to her house and told Mary Jesus had come. Mary, who had submitted during His earlier visit by sitting at His feet to learn, now fell at His feet again. However, because her thoughts limited her belief in His care and concern, she accused Him of not being there to heal her brother.

When Jesus saw the despair in Martha, Mary, and the other friends, their distress deeply moved Him. "Jesus wept."

My friend, the deep emotion Jesus has for us is real. We have a God who cares. He empathizes with our feelings. He sympathizes with compassion, resentment, sorrow, and frustration. He understands our emotions. He cares. "Some of the mourners said, 'See how he loved him!'

These people had seen and heard of Jesus's miracles but still struggled with the incredible power of Christ.

When Jesus went to the tomb of Lazarus, He told them to take away the stone. Martha warned him of the potential "bad odor." Jesus responded, "Did I not tell you that if you believe, you will see the glory of God?" (John 11:40).

Like a foul odor can stop God. I know because my life has stunk worse than a decaying body, and He still uses me for His glory.

Jesus then spoke to God, thanking His Father for listening to His prayer.

Lazarus emerged from the tomb, strips of linen wrapped around his hands, feet, and face. Jesus said, "Take off the grave clothes and let him go" (v. 44). Many of us are spiritually alive but wrapped up in our emotions and thoughts—grave clothes gag and bind.

Jesus also used others to help Him with the healing. He didn't need them to move the stone or take off the grave clothes. He allowed them to participate in the healing.

Fellow believers, we can help one another take off our grave clothes. We are in this together, helping remove burdens and blinders.

Jesus wants us to get rid of what holds us back and to believe His glory can shine. Just because we give our lives to Christ and ask Him into our heart doesn't mean we have rid ourselves of doubt and discouragement. The Enemy, Satan, wants you bound and gagged. Jesus wants you free and speaking His truth.

What are we carrying out of the grave? What have we wrapped ourselves up in that hinders our spiritual growth—discouragement, worry, fear, comparison, anger, loneliness, or other toxic emotional barriers? Are they trailing us, dragging us down, or covering our eyes like tattered grave clothes?

We find security in the words we speak to ourselves. All the unnecessary noise creates meaningless static to our spiritual ears. Capturing every thought, discerning its effect, and deciding to release the adverse effects decreases confusion.

Jesus rescued us from the grave. Let's not carry shreds of the grave clothes with us. Leave behind the bindings and move out in confidence. God is for us. We are important to His plan and His purpose.

Grave clothes keep us in a stagnant spiritual state. Our thoughts should be hemmed in God's love. Capturing the deceptive thoughts of the emotional barriers that bind us and replacing them with God's truth is the beginning of transformation. Clothe yourself with Jesus and His Word.

In learning to release the guilt and deceptive self-talk, we take our first step of faith toward God's plan and purpose. Put off deception. Speak truth.

Deception vs. Truth
Guilty vs. Forgiven
Deception: I have made too many mistakes to be loved by God.

Truth: "For God so loved the world that he gave his one and only Son, that whoever believes in him shall not perish but have eternal life." (John 3:16)

Invisible vs. Seen
Deception: I don't belong here. I have no community or friends.

Truth: "She gave this name to the LORD who spoke to her: 'You are the God who sees me,' for she said, 'I have now seen the One who sees me.'" (Genesis 16:13)

Unimportant vs. Known
Deception: My life is not important.

Truth: "'For I know the plans I have for you,' declares the Lord, 'plans to prosper you and not to harm you, plans to give you hope and a future.'"(Jeremiah 29:11)

"I will be a Father to you, and you will be my sons and daughters, says the Lord Almighty." (2 Corinthians 6:18)

Unwanted vs. Loved
Deception: I am unlovable. No one cares about me.

Truth: "Neither height nor depth, nor anything else in all creation, will be able to separate us from the love of God that is in Christ Jesus our Lord." (Romans 8:39)

Condemned vs. Accepted
Deception: I do not belong.

Truth: I am accepted. "Therefore, there is now no condemnation for those who are in Christ Jesus." (Romans 8:1)

"Yet to all who did receive him, to those who believed in his name, he gave the right to become children of God." (John 1:12)

Cursed vs. Blessed
Deception: I will always be this way because my family is this way. My life is cursed.

Truth: "'The Lord bless you and keep you; the Lord make his face shine on you and be gracious to you; the Lord turn his face toward you and give you peace.'" (Numbers 6:24–26)

Failure vs. Victory

Deception: I am a failure. I can't do anything right.

Truth: "But thanks be to God! He gives us the victory through our Lord Jesus Christ." (1 Corinthians 15:57)

Weak vs. Powerful

Deception: I can't.

Truth: "But he said to me, 'My grace is sufficient for you, for my power is made perfect in weakness.' Therefore, I will boast all the more gladly about my weaknesses, so that Christ's power may rest on me." (2 Corinthians 12:9)

Unclean vs. Pure

Deception: My past is too dirty for me to be called a Christian. I have to be perfect.

Truth: "All who have this hope in him purify themselves, just as he is pure." (1 John 3:3)

Bound vs. Free

Deception: I am stuck. Life will never get any better than this.

Truth: "It is for freedom that Christ has set us free. Stand firm, then, and do not let yourselves be burdened again by a yoke of slavery." (Galatians 5:1)

I hear you say, "Yeah, but . . ." Yeah, but you don't know how messy my life is. You don't understand how stuck I am. You don't see how unlovable I am. If you really knew me . . . Many times we don't feel qualified to take the words and encouragement God gives us in His Word. Today is not that day.

Today we will take one thought captive. Purposefully choose the right thinking. Speak faith. You have greatness waiting to be unleashed. Close your eyes. Visualize the grave clothes being ripped from your spirit and falling at your feet.

The deceptions and truths listed above are not a complete

collection of what you may be saying to yourself. Make your own list. If you're going through the book with a group, you don't have to share the list. Let it be a secret between Jesus and you. But be as transparent as possible with yourself and others. Be merciful and compassionate. Be a restorer, an encourager to yourself and others.

After you make your list, take one thought captive. One at a time. Deception. Name it. Write it. Choose a word of truth to counter it.

The next step is to research what the Bible says about that thought. What is the opposite of what you are thinking? Truth.

There are many ways to search for deceptive thoughts, then find the truth and a scripture to replace them. If you have a study Bible, you can look in the back (the concordance) for specific words. Read the corresponding scripture that tells the truth about the deceptive thought. If you don't have a study Bible, you have the mighty power of the internet or a Bible app.

Filling our minds with God's Word brings us closer to Him. God can fill our mind with His peace if we trust Him, not our thoughts.

Your mind plays an essential part in your spiritual growth. Replace your list of grave clothes—all those emotional barriers that keep you bound—with the words God declares about you. Remove the stink. God's pure love lies beneath.

Sitting on the side of the road leading to my sister's house, I took a deep breath and wiped my tears. Pulling myself together, the best I could, I put the car in Drive and eased my way onto the highway, then took the familiar exit. My heart raced as I came to a halt at the stop sign. Turn right. My mind competed with my rapid heartbeat and took me in new directions of panic.

One thing at a time. One thought at a time. Again, the Lord's voice filled my spirit. Calmness swept over me.

One thing. Drive.

One thought. God is with me.

Arriving at what was left of the house, shock overwhelmed me. Reuniting with family was difficult, but I kept repeating what the Lord had said. *One thing at a time. One thought at a time.*

Over the next couple of weeks, my priority was taking each thought captive. Supernatural Holy Spirit occurrences made that happen. No way the self-control was my doing. I just kept moving forward with one thing and one thought.

Taking each thought captive, I continued to say many recurring things. The words I repeated to myself were hurtful and compromising.

We are all afraid of bullies, but I realized I was my biggest bully. Maybe that's true for you too. Engaging in denigrating internal dialogue builds barriers between Jesus and us.

Each day take one thought captive. Research the truth related to that deception. Most important, have a sense of humor and be compassionate to yourself and others during this process.

According to Dr. Caroline Leaf, author of *Cleaning Up Your Mental Mess*, "It takes 21 days to build a long-term memory, and it takes 63 days to build a new habit."[4]

God didn't create the world and everything in it in one day. He used six days. So we get many more tries, right? Don't quit. Keep going. It is worth it.

Today is Day One. I challenge you to dig into replacing deceptive thoughts with the truth. This step is foundational. It creates a strong base for all that is to come in the distraction detox.

The goal is not only to capture thoughts, replace them with truth, and hold on to the Word. The ultimate intention is to know God's Word, trust in who He is, and believe He wants to do amazing things in and through our lives.

Today is our opportunity to grow. Remove the grave clothes, the emotional barriers, and go. Transformative growth begins here.

---

[4] Caroline Leaf, "It takes 21 days to build a long-term memory," Facebook, December 28, 2018, https://www.facebook.com/drleaf/photos/it-takes-21-days-to-build-a-long-term-memory-and-it-takes-63-days-to-build-a-new/10155793971471078/. Also see *Cleaning Up Your Mental Mess: 5 Simple, Scientifically Proven Steps to Reduce Anxiety, Stress, and Toxic Thinking* (Grand Rapids, MI: Baker Books, 2021).

Detox Challenge

- Always begin with prayer.
- Start with one thing at a time, one thought at a time.
- Make a list of as many deceptive thoughts as possible. Each time you think of another one, capture it on paper. Leave room under each thought to write a truth and a scripture.
- Take one thought per day and research one scriptural truth that dispels the deception.
- Write the scripture under the deception.
- Cross through the deception.
- Use a highlighter to highlight the truth.
- Risk being yourself, the amazing woman God has created you to be.
- Change the question from, What will happen? to What matters?
- With the weapon of God's Word, transformation happens. By Him, not us.

CHAPTER 5
Vertically Challenged

Growing up, I attended a calm and quiet church, but I would sometimes visit churches where people would shout to the Lord or wave their hands in the air. This type of fervent worship scared me, perhaps because I was young and inexperienced. As an adult, I visited a church in which the people worshipped God in a way I had never experienced. They worshipped God with fervor also, but it was different.

The music was upbeat and energetic. The worship band members were smiling with their eyes closed and hands raised—unless they played an instrument.

Peace emanated from their bodies. Joy radiated through their actions. The congregation was very much in control. They were having an intimate personal moment with Jesus. Peace. Joy. Love.

That's what I wanted. I didn't want to feel lonely, unloved, insignificant. I was tired of a life without purpose and passion. After the service, a few people I knew came up and hugged my kids and me. They invited us for coffee in the lobby. We met many friendly people that day. I was skeptical though. I waited to see them act differently in a church setting; I studied every action and critically listened to every word. But they were the same outside the church, on the Little League field, in the local market, or at the playground. They didn't put on a show inside the church. There was something different about them.

A couple of the women invited me and my kids to meet at the playground later that afternoon. The boys and I walked over with a sack full of crunchy snacks and juice boxes. I had a mental list of questions ready. I wanted to know what it was about their faith that seemed so different than what I'd experienced.

Halfway over, I stopped at the corner of the street, waiting for traffic to clear before crossing. I mentally ran through the emotional barriers that kept me from more profound relationships.

- Once they know who I really am, they won't like me.
- They will realize very quickly that I don't have it all together.
- What if they think I'm not a good mother?
- What if they don't like me?
- Will they judge me for my past experiences and turn their backs on me?
- I'm not good enough to be their friend.
- Am I dressed well enough?
- I'm not smart enough to carry on an intelligent conversation with them.

My middle son pulled at my pant leg. "Mom, traffic's cleared. Can we cross?"

My legs wouldn't move. I felt nauseated, panicked. My mind raced, convinced of the validity of my thoughts. I told the boys we needed to go back home. They protested, so we continued toward the playground.

Walking through the park gate, I fought the urge to turn and run, to make an excuse and go home. Before I could come up with a reason to leave, the boys ran toward friends. I heard my name called, turned, and saw the ladies from the church seated at a picnic table—all smiles.

Those smiles will fade once they get to know me.

I walked slowly toward them and sat at the table. We talked and shared for hours. The kids interrupted with calls of unfair play, scraped knees, and requests for more snacks, but we women never lost our place in our shared stories. No one preached, condemned, or judged. We shared serious stories along with a few funny ones.

Some of the women excused themselves to return home, but one of the ladies and I walked over to watch a wild game of Capture the Flag.

"What did you think of the church service today?" she asked.

"It was good." I cautiously responded, not wanting to reveal my judgments or secret desire to know what was different. I wasn't as bold as I'd felt earlier and didn't ask a single one of my prepared questions.

"I hope you come back next Sunday." She gave me a big hug.

I interacted with those women for weeks before I felt secure enough to ask, "What is so different about you? I've known other Christians and attended different churches, but there's something different here."

One woman responded, "I don't know exactly, but one thing I do know is that we love Jesus with our whole heart. Each day my purpose is to fall in love with Him more."

Fall in love with Him more? I thought my heart would explode with that one statement. That is what I wanted. I didn't even know fully what it meant, but I pondered her words. The difference in the women in this church was their deep love for Jesus.

My life had been a struggle of horizontal focus that left me vertically challenged. My love for Jesus hadn't grown because I was too focused on momentary experiences. The toxins I clung to poisoned my spiritual growth.

Fast-forward several years, and here I was, a solid Christian, still struggling with doubt and discouragement. The hinges on my storage chest of self-limiting beliefs creaked from overuse. The backpack I carried into new experiences was heavy with my emotional restrictions.

Taking each thought captive, replacing the deception with truth, and getting down to my bare soul revealed the root of the toxic barriers. My relentless doubt and discouragement were my comfort zone. I continued to carry the jet lag I experienced before. It's hard to break habits.

I needed to be free from the place I was comfortable. Taking each thought captive and replacing it with a scripture was more rote than relational, but the habit was drawing me into the desire to know more about Jesus.

The memory of the love the women at that church had for Jesus resurfaced. I needed to fall deeper in love with Him.

I knew Jesus, read His Word, worked on myself and my relationship with Him, but I kept Him at arm's length. The separation inhibited the connection I needed to overrule my other thoughts. Falling in love with Him more would allow His love to penetrate my heart and soul.

To fall in love with Jesus, I began with prayer, begging God to love me so I could love Him. I soon realized that my doubts about His love came from my self-limiting beliefs. I intellectually knew He loved me but had never truly allowed His love to wash over me completely.

A reminder I've needed many times in my spiritual growth is, it's not all about me. The desire to fall more deeply in love with Jesus sent me back to where I should have been all along—fixated on Him.

Merely obeying the Lord does show our love for Him, but He wants us to long for Him. When we take an active role in detoxing from our mental distractions, we can draw closer to Jesus and find peace of mind. We feel freedom from the restraints and find fulfillment.

During the tragedy my family experienced in 2020, I allowed my rote detox practices to lapse. I was forced into a change I didn't see coming. Remembering to replace my toxic thoughts with scripture helped. As strife roiled, His Word overtook my thoughts.

God will force change in your life if you are not allowing Him to change you. I'm not saying God caused or allowed the tragedy. No matter the cause, I had to decide to partner with God through the aftermath. The fire forced a change of mind.

Many things went wrong during that time. The Enemy was alive and well and threw fiery arrows from multiple directions. Because I had replaced deception with truth, the armor of God was ready and in full strength. When I thought I couldn't make it one more minute, God showed up.

He showed up in the hugs, as social distancing became an afterthought. I saw Him in the dragonflies that covered the property. The double rainbows. The food. The storage trailers when it started to rain. The hundreds of helping hands.

Prayer, a conversation with Jesus, was constant. I prayed for my family, for the strangers who drove by and stopped to give donations. *God, you are so good.*

In the most challenging time in my life, my love for Jesus has sustained me above anything else. During that time, I fell in love with Jesus more.

Fixing our eyes on Jesus, the pioneer and perfecter of faith. For the joy set before him, he endured the cross, scorning its shame, and sat down at the right hand of the throne of God. Consider him who endured such opposition from sinners, so that you will not grow weary and lose heart.
—Hebrews 12: 2–3

"Fixing our eyes on Jesus." A vertical stare. Falling in love with Jesus requires constant focus on Him—even when life and our thoughts are challenging, chaotic, and distracting.

Hebrews 11 shows us faith in action. Hebrews 12 instructs us on how to accomplish that in the first few verses.

Do you remember when you were little and your birthday was getting close? You felt excited and anxious. (To tell the truth, I still feel this way when a birthday is coming.) We celebrate. We know we will be getting or giving a special gift or sweet treat.

Our faith is similar. Two words describe faith: *confidence* and *assurance*. We have a secure beginning and ending point. The beginning point is believing in God's character, confident He is who He says He is. The endpoint is believing in God's promises, the assurance He will do what He says He will do.

When we believe that God will fulfill His promises even though we don't see those promises materializing, that is true faith. Getting to know the creator and the promise keeper increases our love for Him.

Hebrews 12 begins with the image of "a great cloud of witnesses," the Jewish faith Hall of Fame. Their faithfulness is a constant encouragement to us. We do not struggle without proof of God's character and promises. These believers wrestled with the same root problems we have today.

Mary of Magdalene was with Jesus during His ministry and through His crucifixion and His burial. Three days after He was placed in the tomb, she returned to it and saw that the stone no longer covered the entrance. Filled with terror, she ran to the house where the disciples were hiding. She feared the Romans had taken Jesus's body.

A couple of disciples rushed to the tomb, inspected what remained, and saw only the linen strips that had covered Jesus's body.

Mary returned to the tomb, filled with sadness. She began to weep, then two angels appeared and asked why she was crying.

When Mary turned, she saw a man. She believed him to be the gardener. She begged him to tell her where Jesus's body had been taken. Mary saw the truth of the resurrection but did not recognize it.

• Then Jesus called her by name.

Her gaze fixed on Him, and she realized it was Jesus. She "cried out in Aramaic, 'Rabboni!' (which means Teacher)," and worshipped Him. She then returned to the disciples and told them everything she had seen.

Jesus later appeared to the disciples in the house where they were sequestered. "Peace be with you." He showed them His hands and side—

proof of the death He endured and His resurrection. The disciples had felt terror, despair, and sadness when Jesus died. But when they saw the resurrected Jesus, they felt peace and joy.

The Christian life is hard work. To live effectively, we must keep our eyes on Jesus. When we look away, we feel lonely, discouraged, and doubtful. Keeping our eyes vertical allows our love for Him to grow. We gain confidence and assurance.

Hebrews 12 presents proof of who Jesus is and what He can and will do in and through our lives. Jesus alone can forgive our sins. We can find true peace and real meaning in our lives when we believe in Him. Learning more about Jesus solidifies our belief. Knowing Him better increases our trust in Him. With trust comes love. With love comes action.

To love Jesus more, we have to throw off everything that hinders and all that entangles us (Hebrews 12:1). Those emotional barriers we have built must be discarded. With every deception replaced by truth, we throw off that which hinders.

God has marked out a race for us. He has a plan. He has given us a purpose. Our purpose is to glorify Him in all that we say, do, and are. To fulfill our purpose and His plan, we must persevere. Jesus enables us to keep going, to overcome difficulties, and to reach the destiny He desires for us.

Self-limiting beliefs and thoughts put the focus on us. Fixing our gaze on Jesus takes the horizontal focus off ourselves and redirects it vertically. A vertical gaze repositions our obsession with God-restricting actions and leads to freedom. Freedom to praise the Lord. "Let everything that has breath, praise the Lord" (Psalm 150:6).

We may not like what's going on around us. It may feel uncomfortable. What-ifs, inadequacy, and discouragement may seem all-consuming. Changing our horizontal focus to the One who is in control places our focus in the proper alignment.

How does this relate to falling in love with Jesus? The more attention we give Him, the better we know Him and understand who

He is. Our wisdom about what He desires to do in and through us increases, and our love for Him grows.

We have to be freed from the place we find comfort and the bad habits we've created in our minds. Our love for Jesus is the gateway to true freedom.

Appreciating God for what He has done and what He will do resets our baseline of love. We are set free when these deceptive thoughts are released.

Day by day, hour by hour, take those thoughts captive. Replace them with scripture. Release your horizontal grip, and raise your mind vertically to receive Jesus's love.

We can get there if we let go of what we are holding tight to. When forced to let go of everything we think we control, we are free to receive all that Christ has for us. We are not letting go of responsibilities; we are releasing our grip on what we never had control over.

Let go of the so-called normal. Receive the new. Accept the love Jesus has for you. Increase the love you have for Him. Be transformed.

Conforming to the old way, the normal we knew, is the wrong way to live. Most people live in a horizontal perspective. Christians live with a vertical point of view.

Transformation occurs from the inside out—a direct, vertical connection to the One who is sovereign over all.

Discarding the unnecessary opens an opportunity to receive Jesus's love. How do you fall more in love with Him? Learn who He is. Fix your eyes on Him.

Who is He, and what does He promise? Here is a list of some of His attributes and His promises.

God Protects

"The Lord is my rock, my fortress, and my deliverer; my God is my rock, in whom I take refuge, my shield and the horn of my salvation, my stronghold" (Psalm 18:2).

God's protection of His people is limitless. David, the author of many psalms, characterized God's care with five military symbols:

(1) a rock that can't be moved by anyone who would harm us; (2) a fortress, a place of safety, where the Enemy cannot attack; (3) a shield that defends us from injury; (4) a horn of salvation, the symbol of might and power; (5) a stronghold high above our enemies. He is our protector.

God Provides

"Everything that lives and moves about will be food for you. Just as I gave you the green plants, I now give you everything" (Genesis 9:3).

God gives us so many blessings. He created the universe and gave food to every living thing. He provides for our physical, spiritual, emotional, and community needs. He provides rest when we trust in Him. He gives eternal life when we believe in Him. He offers peace, comfort, direction, and grace—free to all who believe.

God Forgives

"For he has rescued us from the dominion of darkness and brought us into the kingdom of the Son he loves, in whom we have redemption, the forgiveness of sins" (Colossians 1:13–14).

Jesus rescued us (believers) from the domain of darkness and brought us into the kingdom. We were under Satan's rule, slaves to him and to sin. But Jesus provided redemption. Through His atoning death, He purchased our freedom. He granted us forgiveness of sins and gave us citizenship in His kingdom. His forgiveness is a gift of grace. We are not worthy of His forgiveness, but He gave it anyway.

God Has All Authority

"Moses said to God, 'Suppose I go to the Israelites and say to them, "The God of your fathers has sent me to you," and they ask me, "What is his name?" Then what shall I tell them?' God said to Moses, 'I am who I am. This is what you are to say to the Israelites: "I am has sent me to you"'" (Exodus 3:13–14).

God calls himself I am, a name describing His eternal power and unchangeable character. In a world where values, morals, and laws change frequently, we can find stability and security in our unchanging God. He is in control and has authority over all.

God Is Good

"You, Lord, are forgiving and good, abounding in love to all who call to you" (Psalm 86:5).

Many scriptures proclaim God's goodness. Look up the word *goodness* in the concordance of your study Bible or do a word search on a Bible website. Which verse about God's goodness resonates most with you? In Psalm 86, David appeals to God for help. He states his need for God, his submission to God, and his dependence on God. He is confident of God's character and knows the Lord is good.

Sometimes our pain, doubt, and discouragement are so great that all we can do is cry out to God. When there seems to be no relief, we have to rely on the knowledge of His greatness. The fact is, He works for the good of all who believe because He is good.

God Is Love

"This is love: not that we loved God, but that he loved us and sent his Son as an atoning sacrifice for our sins" (1 John 1:10).

Love explains why God creates. He creates because He loves. He creates people to love one another. God is love. He expresses His love to us forever.

Our horizontal view of shallow and selfish thoughts has turned these words around and contaminated our understanding of love. Many people think love is what makes a person feel good. That's not real love. Real love is like God—holy, just, and perfect.

God Is a Peace-Giver

Jesus said, "Peace I leave with you; my peace I give you. I do not give to you as the world gives. Do not let your hearts be troubled, and do not be afraid" (John 14:27).

The result of the Holy Spirit's work in our lives is a deep, everlasting peace. God's peace is not like the world's. Its definition of peace is lack of conflict. Christ's peace is a confident assurance in any circumstance that God is present and working out His goodwill. His peace drives away fear. Jesus says He will give us His peace if we choose to accept it. He is the Prince of Peace. Accept His offer.

God Is Alive

Paul wrote, "I have been crucified with Christ and I no longer live, but Christ lives in me. The life I now live in the body, I live by faith in the Son of God, who loved me and gave himself for me" (Galatians 2:20).

When we accept Christ as our Savior, we become one with Him. We have unity with Him. Our old lives die. We are forgiven, and given new life. The Holy Spirit lives in us. We are no longer alone. He is our power for living and our hope for the future. He is alive!

God Fulfills His Promises

"Let us hold unswervingly to the hope we profess, for he who promised is faithful" (Hebrews 10:23).

God is the God of promises. He promises to be with us, give us strength, and comfort us. He promises compassion, hope, peace, joy, and a future. He fulfills every promise. Let's not get His promises and our desires mixed up. He doesn't give us everything we want, but He promises to provide what we need.

God Is Sovereign over All

"For in him all things were created: things in heaven and on earth, visible and invisible, whether thrones or powers or rulers or authorities; all things have been created through him and for him" (Colossians 1:16).

The apostle Paul explained that God created all the rulers, powers, thrones, and authorities of the spiritual and the physical worlds. All are under the authority of Christ, who has no equal and no rival. He is Lord of all.

Reading scripture and believing who God is and what He promises develop the baseline in our hearts, minds, and souls. Our vertical relationship with Jesus grows as we learn more about Him, and it also takes our focus off of our horizontal experience.

Horizontal challenges are the difficulties we have when we concentrate on ourselves or the opinions of others. When our gaze peers around the surface of the earth, our eyes are taken off of Jesus. Improving our vertical sight affirms the truth of God's love for us and increases our love for Him. The more we look toward Jesus, the more we admire Him. As we better understand the sacrifice He made, the promises He keeps, and the love He offers, we are transformed. The more we know, the more we continue to fall in love with Jesus. When we fix our gaze on Him, we prioritize His work in our lives.

Love the Lord your God with all your heart, all your mind, and all your soul. Set your gaze on Him.

Detox Challenge

- Always begin with prayer: "Lord, I want to fall more in love with you."
- Read the truth replacements from chapter 4.
- Reread the scripture in this chapter that reveals who God is and what He promises.
- Research other promises that align with your needs.
- Choose one scripture that the Lord puts on your heart. Write it on a few sticky notes and place them where you will see them throughout the day.
- Try to memorize the scripture. I'm not great at remembering, so I try to familiarize myself with the verse and understand what God is saying to me.
- Continue to take self-limiting, God-restricting thoughts captive each day. Write them down.
- Repeat the process from chapter 4 as the thoughts arise. Replace each thought with scripture.
- Write these four statements beneath your truth for today.
  - I am accepted in Christ.
  - I am secure in Christ.
  - I am significant in Christ.
  - I am loved.

CHAPTER 6
Feeling the Feels

As David and I raised our boys, I strongly encouraged them to express their feelings. I meant verbally, but that is not how they always translated my words.

Classic example. Snow began to fall in the evening, just after dinner. The boys wanted to go out and play. I held off as long as I could, finally letting them go out for an hour before bath and bed. As often happens with kids, someone did something to someone, and they became angry. I demanded that all three boys come into the house. They bathed and went to their separate rooms for the night.

The one who felt wronged stewed all night long. The next morning, he was up and out of bed early. He ate his breakfast, put on his winter garb, and went outside. His brothers soon followed. The snowballs hit the door as they opened it. Snow and ice covered the floor. I yelled, pulled the targeted son back in the door, and stormed toward the bombardier. He threw a snowball with immense power, hitting me in the face.

He stood stunned. I was not laughing. He defended himself. I didn't utter a word, just pointed toward the house as I scraped snow from my hair, nightgown, and flip-flopped feet. He continued to tell me it wasn't his fault. He'd been the one wronged the previous night, and this was his vengeance. I formulated my revenge on him as I walked into the house.

My son fumed as he undressed and stormed upstairs. The targeted child stood there, teary-eyed, as blood trickled down his cheek. Apparently, when I pushed by him to get to the rapid-fire thrower, he scraped his face on the screen door.

I chuckle now, but at the time, I was not amused. I became defensive and told my son he should have backed away and moved so I could get out the door—another moment I've failed as a mother. I cleaned the scrape with a napkin from the breakfast table and helped him undress. His face grew redder and redder.

"Are you cold?" I asked.

"No, I'm mad as . . ."

Whoa. That escalated. I took a step back. My earlier response hadn't been good. I shouldn't have blamed him for not getting out of the way. After addressing his foul language, I looked him in the eye and apologized for being angry and blaming him earlier.

He smiled.

I made him hot chocolate, put on a movie for him and the youngest, and walked upstairs.

The bedroom door was ajar, and I heard punching. When I peeked through the crack, I saw my son punching a pillow. We'd taught our boys to hit a cushion instead of one another.

"What's going on?" I asked.

"He made me fall last night when he pushed me on the driveway." He growled.

"And revenge was your first thought?"

"Well." He sat on the bed contemplating what I'd asked.

I've been there. When I think I've been wronged or taken advantage of, I get angry. My reactions paved the way for the experience. I do not like people doing wrong to me, my family, or my friends. Fire burns in me when others are taken advantage of, especially if they are underprivileged, poor, or uneducated.

My son gave me the details of what had happened just before I called them in. "I tried to tell you, but you were too focused on getting us to bed."

His anger festered. He didn't take the thought captive or discern right from wrong, deception from truth. Because I had a plan, I hadn't listened to him to help him make the right decision.

Anger wasn't a feeling David and I tried to teach our children. We encouraged peace and talking things out, not fury and revenge-filled snowball attacks. But I didn't listen to my son's feelings and he shut down. He felt as though he'd been taken advantage of, and he reacted in anger rather than hitting pause. He let his thoughts get away from him and chose to seek revenge rather than turn away.

It seems like a lot to expect a child to respond rather than react. But isn't childhood when we need to learn positive habits and responses rather than relearn hurtful patterns?

I had reacted to his response, and the labels I put on myself piled up. *I'm a bad mom. I always knew I would be.* My feelings became my priority. Regulating my emotions hadn't been a significant focus for me.

How many times do we determine and evaluate a feeling in the wrong way? How many times do we just do what we always do?

My state of anxiety became a habit, and it hindered my journey with the Lord.

I am not only my biggest bully; I'm also my worst enemy. One wrong decision led to negative behaviors. Distractions pull us emotionally, spiritually, and physically.

I don't want to make all feelings out to be negative. Some protect us from danger. But not all feelings are okay. Discerning between the real feelings and the wrong feelings creates a preemptive habit that helps us turn to God to receive the peace He offers.

Toxic feelings build barriers in our spiritual life. They create tension. The tension creates reactions. Reactions create walls. Walls separate spiritual connections. Spiritual jet lag sets in.

Spiritual jet lag—the confusion caused by the emotional barriers—and the feelings associated with my responses led to a muddled understanding of how to overcome doubt and discouragement. Layering self-limiting behaviors caused God-limiting actions.

Emotional reactions limited what I thought God could do in and through me. I confess that I allowed the feelings I had in response to the barriers to take residency. I dreaded the process of feeling the real feelings. Even the thought of capturing a thought made me anxious: do I want to feel what that thought causes?

I gave those toxic thoughts a home rather than discerning what feelings created my confusion. I needed to pause, not stop. Pause and feel the feelings, then decide if the feeling deserves more attention. Is God stretching me to grow, or am I creating a new bad habit? I'm not good at taking the time to feel, pause, and listen. For me, it's more like feel, escalate the feeling, and react to the feeling.

Spiritual jet lag may be more prevalent during certain seasons of life. And I have had many different seasons over the years. My reactions in those seasons resulted in terrible decisions and habits. Patterns emerged and increased stress in my faith journey.

My most significant role change happened when my youngest was finishing high school. The empty nest was the most frightening change because I believed it would be my big break to serve God in an impactful way. I wouldn't have to referee snowball fights and pillow punching anymore.

I was finally getting my chance to be who God called me to be. I could fulfill all the dreams and desires I held tight before raising our children. I opened the door to opportunities where I thought I was capable—longtime dreams, freedom, options, and opportunities. I prayed and began to push ahead in the direction I wanted to go.

But I was filled with anxiety. I had waited for my turn, and now I was overwhelmed with the emotions that flooded into my spirit. Discontent. Doubt. Confusion. *I can't. I'm not prepared.* I reopened my storage chest of self-limiting beliefs.

I searched for my purpose and calling while we raised our children. I knew God had called me to speak and teach His Word and share the lessons I had learned. That was my call. My purpose during the childrearing years had been to prepare for this season. So why the anxiety?

Did I hear His call? Had I wasted twenty-plus years waiting to fulfill His purpose and calling, or had I been doing His will all along and hadn't seen it?

My passion burned to help others see who God was, to see who He created us to be and what He's calling us to do. What could I do with that fire? What did God want me to do with the calling He'd laid on my heart? Was this another season of disappointment? I didn't allow myself to feel what was real, so I created negative responses.

I convinced myself I had no place writing or speaking into women's lives. There was bitterness and anger. I don't like thinking about that season now because the anxiety reappears with each memory. My focus was on failure rather than discerning the feelings and making a wise decision about each one.

I had no peace in my spirit, and I allowed many of the negative feelings to take up residence in my storage chest of self-limiting beliefs—restrictions on what I could do. I constructed sturdy walls of doubt and deep discouragement.

I'm so proud of the men our sons have become. They actually like us! All three have an incredible work ethic. Each chose a career in baseball but have different jobs. They like one another and talk numerous times during the week.

The world continues to tell us to work and strive for success. I have found great peace and joy in helping women grow spiritually, walking alongside them as a friend and guiding them closer to Jesus.

God's peace is different from the world's peace. True peace is not found in positive thinking, the absence of conflict, or good feelings. It comes from knowing God is in control.

What is burning inside you? What are you passionate about? When you find those two things and allow yourself to feel the real feeling without others' opinions or advice interfering, you will find peace. Cast all your cares on the Lord.

How do you respond in a healthy way?

When I didn't take my thoughts captive, I reacted. Did I do all things right as a mom? No. Was my identity in baseball? No. My reactions led to terrible decisions. When I allowed myself to feel the feeling, then thought through the responses, I grew closer to God. Now I live a joyous life. If I pause, I can discern if thoughts are deceptive, not real, but I have to allow myself to feel the confusion before I respond.

Feel the negative emotions, but let them go if they make a bed and settle into your deceptive category.

The perception of failure, success, or lack of value distracts us from God's promises. Anxiety and numbness build if we refuse to feel.

Do not be anxious about anything, but in every situation, by prayer and petition, with thanksgiving, present your requests to God. And the peace of God, which transcends all understanding, will guard your hearts and your minds in Christ Jesus.

–Philippians 4:6–7

Imagine never feeling anxious. It seems impossible. Paul, the author of Philippians, knew we would experience uncomfortable and chaotic situations. This book is Paul's joy letter to his friends, the believers in Philippi. The concept of rejoicing or joy appears sixteen times in four chapters. Again and again, Paul encourages believers to rejoice.

We have a lot to learn from Paul. People today want to be successful, and when we are not, we shut down because of negative feelings. Then anxiety builds.

Paul encourages believers to stand firm in the Lord. How do we do that? In chapter five, we talked about our vertical relationship with the Lord rather than our horizontal focus on the world. Easy to say, but hard to do at times.

The way to stand firm is to keep our eyes on Christ. Focus on the fact that Christ has everything under His control. Standing firm means resisting negative thoughts. It means persevering when we doubt and feel discouraged.

Does it seem strange that a man in prison would tell a church to rejoice and share joy? Paul was full of joy because he knew that no matter what happened to him, Jesus was with him. We can easily get discouraged about unpleasant circumstances or feelings. Ultimate joy comes from Christ dwelling in us. He will fulfill His purposes for us.

How do we find joy? Joy is the opposite of anxiety. When our feelings are under God's control, we have peace. Peace comes when we feel the feelings but don't let them control our reactions and response. We learn to control the uncomfortable feelings, accept the Lord's peace, and experience His joy.

How do we experience the great joy Paul speaks of in Philippians? "Do not be anxious." Another easier-said-than-done statement. The feelings causing apprehension keep us from experiencing peace.

Being anxious about nothing seems impossible. To experience great joy, we take control of our anxiety with God's help. Paul advises believers to pray "in every situation."

Do you want to be less anxious? Pray more.

Do you want the ability to pause and discern the feeling that is real versus the counterfeit one? Pray.

When we are filled with dread and other uncomfortable emotions, we do not find peace in them. Pausing to feel the emotion, accept the concern, and discern the response helps guide us to God's peace and joy.

People want to be happy, but the circumstances of life toss and turn us because of successes, failures, and inconveniences. The thought of happiness can evoke the good feelings of walking hand in hand with someone we love, sitting on a beach with the sun shining and the waves rolling, receiving a special gift, or laughing with a group of good friends. Peace in success. Joy in success.

True peace is not found in fame and fortune. Peace isn't found in materials or in the positive thinking of others. It isn't found in the absence of conflict. Good feelings don't produce peace. True peace comes from knowing God is in control, not our feelings.

Too often, though, we define success by our happiness. We chase this elusive ideal thinking money, acceptance, popularity, or a bigger house will maintain this happiness. Then the money is gone, someone rejects us, we aren't invited to the party, the house isn't what we thought it would be. Happiness flees, despair enters.

God gives us peace, but we must hold on to it. We don't want to lose the peace in the next hour or experience. Dwell in it.

Feel it. Don't let it stay if it makes you want to react. Acknowledge the deception, then redeem it with truth. Stop the lies you tell yourself in response to the doubtful or dubious feeling.

Prayer can be frustrating. When we don't see immediate results, we doubt God's presence and His desire to help us. Thinking that way causes us to miss how prayer works. Prayer opens relational communication with God. Talk with God in an open way.

Prayer is the umbrella word; underneath it are *petition* and *thanksgiving*. A petition is a humble, earnest plea for a specific need for something significant. You admit you cannot overcome the feeling you have in response to an emotional blockade you unearth without God's help.

Thanksgiving is the acknowledgment of what is right and good about God. Thankfulness is tied to who God is. Giving thanks is not always at the top of our minds when we make a request to God.

It is difficult to be grateful when we don't know the outcome, when we are not in control. But Paul tells us to give thanks—not for the problem but for the God we invite into our pain.

God wants us to make our meek and humble requests with thanksgiving. Be honest about your feelings, and be thankful for who God is before you know the outcome of your prayer.

When we pray this way, we can expect God to give us His peace, "which transcends all understanding," to guard our heart and mind.

We can experience calm in the chaos. We know God hears our prayers because His peace fills us. Embrace the peace. Rest.

Our circumstances may not change, but we will. God's peace surpasses all understanding because we can't comprehend its existence, but we can feel its presence. It's as though God puts an army of soldiers around our feelings and thoughts. He protects us from escalating anxiety and reactionary responses.

What you allow into your mind determines what comes out in your thoughts, feelings, and actions. Program your mind to focus on what is of God. To change your anxiety into peace, present your feelings to God. Then learn to feel the ones that frighten you. Peace of mind begins with validating and evaluating your feelings, then your reactions to the emotions. When you feel anxiety rising, reactions bubbling, and unrighteous responses brewing, take these four steps to gain peace of mind.

- Pause when you feel the tension. Experience the feeling. Discern deception versus truth.
- Stop the lies you tell yourself, building their believability. Identify the feeling, then take the thought captive and prioritize the importance of truth. Stopping the untruth before it fills the storage chest of self-limiting beliefs takes you closer to God's peace and joy.
- Surrender the feeling to God in prayer. Your anxiety will decrease when you release a feeling that is not the truth and not of God.
- Expect the peace and joy that is beyond all understanding. God wants what's best. Peace is best.

Evaluating the emotional barriers we've built helps us move toward terminating the toxins. As we continue the detox process, don't rush past one step to get to the next. Spend time in prayer and stillness before God to understand and embrace the process.

I know you can do this. God is with you, and I am praying for you.

Detox Challenge

- Always begin with prayer.
- Take one thought captive.
- How does it make you feel?
- Hit pause and ponder the feeling.
- Question your feeling.
- Is this feeling one that is going to help me grow closer to the Lord?
- Am I letting this feeling take root?
- Am I ready to react or listen to guidance?
- Pray. Open up relational communication with the Lord. Invite Him in.
- Petition: Make your humble request for the Lord to help you press pause on the feeling as you uncover the emotional barriers. Ask Him to help you move forward, not shut down because of doubt or discouragement.
- Thankfulness: Thank Him for who He is and who He has created you to be in Him. Thank Him in advance for what He is doing in and through you.
- Feel the real feeling of peace, peace beyond all understanding.
- Allow peace to guard your heart and mind.
- Allow joy to be your goal.

CHAPTER 7

Removal Process

Terminating toxins takes time and focus. With our vertical gaze fixed on Jesus, we know we are not alone as we rid ourselves of the toxins. Validating and evaluating our feelings and reactions to our emotions help identify and remove three serious toxins. When we get rid of those, we can have a healthier, more fulfilling life.

Every year, without fail, I got sick after the holidays, starting with stuffy sinuses, which escalated into an asthma attack. Somewhere between the stuffiness and the attack, the pressure in my ears increased, as did the ringing, which led to a double ear infection. Equilibrium issues made me feel like I was standing in a body of water, the waves tossing me in one direction then another.

A few months earlier, my doctor had told me that some of my recurring symptoms were food-related. I ignored her warnings. Food sensitivities are challenging. I didn't want to know.

Our family was familiar with food sensitivities. At nine weeks old, our second son, Charley, turned blue at my breast. After several months and a comprehensive round of testing, the medical team determined he was sensitive to the food I ate. He was exposed to the allergens through my breast milk.

The limited diet I adhered to was more than restrictive of food. I could name the items allowed on less than ten fingers—more than basic.

I consumed large amounts of a small number of food items but continued to lose too much weight. Charley thrived, but I melted away. My priority was my son's life, not my own. I could sacrifice food and more for him to grow.

I had to repeat the same diet when our third son, Will, was born. Each time I stripped our shelves of all the foods I usually consumed—the good-tasting items. I wasn't allowed to eat anything processed, from boxes or cans. They all contained one or more items the babies couldn't tolerate. All were my comfort foods.

No more chips, crackers, or cookies. Snacks were off-limits. Healthy people say, "It's so good for you to eat this way." But when you have nine items you can eat, with salt as the only seasoning, meal time gets boring. How healthy can such a restrictive diet be?

The monotony of eating the same items daily made me sad. My taste buds begged for something challenging—pepper, hot sauce, lemon, vinegar, pickles, or salty chips. Anything that could perk up my taste buds, make my tongue tingle and my mouth water.

I stuck it out and limited my diet. For my kids, I can do anything. But when it came to making that decision for myself, it was a bit harder to accept. I wanted the bad stuff, the unhealthy foods. I can even argue that my mental health is at risk when I eliminate eating for fun.

Years later, when I walked into the doctor's office—barely able to breathe, dizzy, and in pain—I wasn't ready to accept that I could have sensitivities similar to the boys'. Accepting the reality wouldn't be easy.

The doctor confirmed her suspicions with blood testing for food allergies and sensitivities. The first test revealed fifty-four items of sensitivity. The medical advice was to detox from all the food items for six to eight weeks.

My husband and I inspected the list of culprits when I returned home. We analyzed the suggestions of items to eliminate. Tears poured down my cheeks at the sacrifice I was required to make.

- Would it help?
- Would I feel better?
- Could I balance a healthy diet with all those foods eliminated?
- How on earth could I travel and avoid all those foods?

I made a mental list of reasons the strict diet wouldn't work. The testing isn't valid. I cannot be sensitive to all these foods. My symptoms have to be related to another issue.

The asthma attack along with the sinus and ear infections weren't the only symptoms. I had been gaining unexplained weight. Some days I didn't want to get out of bed due to extreme fatigue. My body ached all the time. I had severe joint pain.

At one point, David was concerned I was depressed because there were no apparent reasons for all the issues. He was kind, though, when he reminded me of all the symptoms and encouraged me to try the restricted diet. "What do you have to lose?"

I cried. A sense of doom engulfed me.

I stripped the cabinets of all the forbidden items. Poor David hid some of his favorite snacks and candies. I was like a rabid dog going after unhealthy items. I used pity, guilt, and shame to get him to share.

The next grocery store run was more expensive than usual because of the amount of food I bought. I made sure I had enough of what I could eat. The extra supplies took up the cabinet space of the former items. I wanted to run, thinking about how sad removing the foods made me.

I've done a few bouts of detoxing from sugar and other not-so-healthy items, stripping away the bad to add the good. The process was hard. I needed the sugar and junk. Don't even ask about flour, my favorite ingredient.

One night during the cleansing process, I lay in bed praying for God to heal me so I could go back to eating what I wanted. His whisper in my spirit reminded me I could continue to eat those foods, but they were killing my body. I could choose to sacrifice my desires for harmful items and replenish my cells with healthy nourishment. Only with the Holy Spirit's help could I detox the bad food.

As I consumed only the healthy items, my body revolted. My stomach reacted harshly. My body shook, my head pounded. Every morning I awoke with a fogginess that made me unsteady. Why was I doing this? Nothing changed.

I reminded myself it was a process: one step, one choice, one day at a time.

Within one week, my symptoms decreased. Ten days passed. I felt like an entirely new woman. I don't think I had ever felt that good in my entire life. I was stunned. My mind cleared, my attitude grew joyful, and my energy increased—all new experiences. Within six weeks, I felt like a different person.

After a few years of dealing with my food sensitivities, I see the damage a little exposure does. Grains give me acne and make my joints ache. Corn and corn products cause sinus and ear infections. Egg whites give me flaming red, raised hives. I could name a lot more, but you get the idea.

When I identified the emotional barriers and the feelings, releasing them was hard. Even though I knew the change was for my own good, I couldn't let go of the many barriers I held dear.

Unhealthy emotional barricades block the path for good. Terminating the identified emotional toxins may be the most challenging part, but it's essential. I tended to struggle when other toxins arose in different seasons. As I thought I had a handle on shame from the past, a memory would attack, and down the path to the darkness I went.

It was much like walking to the pantry and finding it empty, then going to the grocery store and picking up something I knew I shouldn't have. I picked up old unhealthy habits.

You used to walk in these ways, in the life you once lived. But now you must also rid yourselves of all such things as these: anger, rage, malice, slander, and filthy language from your lips.

–Colossians 3:7–8

One subject that leads to a heated discussion related to Jesus and the Bible is sin. Sin is a difficult concept to wrap our minds around. The word *sin*, or the list of sins in the Bible, doesn't create agitation. Instead, the discomfort surrounding the word leads to anxiety.

Sin is the thoughts, words, and actions by which humans rebel against God, miss His purpose for their lives, and surrender to the power of evil. When we focus on sin, no matter our personal view of its severity, we are separated from Christ. Sin is anything that takes our focus from God and causes us to miss His purpose for our life or our calling.

Realizing our distorted understanding of what's evil and our justification of how others' sins are worse than ours will help us see what's holding us back. Our desire to reveal it, remove it, and move forward becomes our reality.

Unfortunately, many Christians live in the chaos of trying to figure out what separates them from a loving God. We believe we have habits we cannot control. If we don't change our thoughts and remove the emotional barriers, we will not experience spiritual transformation. Our minds need to be renewed, retrained.

We have a new identity in Christ. Our minds will determine our well-being. If we continue to cling to the habits, emotional barriers, and discouragement just because we always have, we cannot reach the potential of what Christ wants to do in and through us. We excuse our sins with the rationalization, "This is just the way I am." But God calls us to live from the new perspective. Christ is to be the focus of our life.

We cannot stop there. Even though we have heavenly blessings available to us through Christ, we must access them by obeying God's Word. Kick out the earthly perspective. Don't give it fresh soil to take root.

The scripture above lists common sins. These need to be removed permanently. We have been raised and seated with Christ (Colossians 3:1). Our spiritual life is full of Him when we accept His Holy Spirit.

Why exchange the royal reign of Christ in our lives for an impoverished spiritual mentality? We can remove the emotional chains, put to death the sins of our earthly nature. They don't belong in our life. Jesus has cleansed us by His blood, His sacrifice. Instead of wearing the grave clothes of the old self, replace them with the new. If we continue to replenish our souls with deceptive and counterfeit thoughts, we make our souls dirty, adding more grave clothes. We can cultivate a fresh, new spirit.

In previous chapters, we've discussed the emotional barricades and the emotions that arise and cause anxiety. Remember the feelings we need to gain control over? As we begin to remove the barriers, they will resurface.

Be aware and take those emotions under control as we talk through these sins and distractions. Never let the barriers keep you from accepting what God wants to do in and through you.

I don't know all the terrible circumstances you've experienced, the lies you have convinced yourself are real, or the feelings that led you to doubt and discouragement. What I can do is give you a list you can review and then let the Lord guide you to the removal—cleaning off the shelves and emptying your self-limiting storage chest.

Like organizing cabinets during a food cleanse, mute the noise of emotional barriers. Give up all the adverse reactions, thoughts, and obstacles preventing you from accepting God's best. Defining the obstacles allows you to acknowledge the obstructions in your life.

The process is not a one-and-done. We continue the process as other toxins appear in different seasons of our lives. God only reveals what we can handle each time. He is with us.

What are you willing to give up, and how do you begin?

Are you ready to start the process? Ready or not, here we go. Start with a few small steps. It's difficult to remove the toxins, but I promise the process is worth it and results in peace. The Lord rejoices as the work begins. Let's begin together.

When I began writing this chapter, I jumped on social media and asked, "I need your help. I'm writing my second book, and I talk about the distractions keeping us from a deeper relationship with the Lord.

Not external distractions but internal ones like shame, lack of worth, or comparison. What others can you add that I don't have here?"

I was blown away by the transparency and answers. I was also shocked by the number of individuals who shared their distractions and stories. Thank you for trusting me with them. I prayed for every person who responded.

The list from the responses was extensive. After looking over it, I found there were three categories, which will help us remove the toxins: (1) fear, (2) unbelief, and (3) guilt and shame. Anger, jealousy, and worry are by-products of the barriers in the categories, not core toxins.

I've included the most prevalent toxins for each category, with some overlapping in the groups. A few may apply to you when you first read them. Some may emerge later. A couple may catch your attention, but you may not be convinced they apply to you. Others may stick in your mind as you read through them.

Read them with an open mind, checking the root not your reactions.

Fear

The first core toxin is fear, which causes us to fight, freeze, or flee because of our unease. Frightful fear, or fearfulness is not the spirit given to us by God (2 Timothy 1:7). The Enemy loves to keep us entangled.

The fears range from lack of trust in God, others, and ourselves to fearing failure. A few responders talked about the fear of success, selfish ambition, and needing to be productive. This category includes the fear of being unable to maintain what we think we should be doing, of working for titles and notoriety, and of not being able to do it all.

The core toxin appears in comparison, concern about what others think, and self-centered competition. These are fear-driven personal desires. We also fear the possibility of health issues—what may come, what has been diagnosed, or what may be incurable. Some other internal blocks are the fear of being a good wife or mom as well as the fear of never experiencing those blessings. We also fear the future.

The concern of external danger overwhelms our ability to connect or take a chance on an adventure or opportunity.

Fear was the primary toxin in my life. I feared everything. Laced with worry, fear was my go-to emotion. My detrimental reactions and responses were all rooted in fear.

Unbelief

Unbelief is the second core toxin. I was shocked to realize unbelief is related to disobedience, a condition of being unpersuadable—stuck in our ways. It denotes the obstinate rejection of God's will. Our unbelief separates us from what God desires to do in and through us, the "immeasurably more" than we can even imagine.

The toxin of not being good enough is one most women struggle with, but many men also expressed their concern about not being enough. Unbelief robs us of self-confidence. We experience a sense of being unloved and lacking value. We doubt God and self. Unbelief leads to discouragement and loneliness.

Questioning the validity of the Bible and our ability to understand what it means breaks our spiritual connection to God. We may be perplexed by how ancient teachings relate to us. We may doubt that a loving God could love people like us. We feel confused, unsure of our calling or purpose.

Frustration occurs when we can't figure out why bad things happen to good people or why good things happen to bad people. Spiritual isolation results when our pride overtakes His will. We rely on our desires instead.

We may try to do all the right things in the correct order and without error. We want to control rather than release power to Jesus. We deny that God can do more and do it better than we ever could. We don't accept the fact that God has our best interest in mind.

Guilt and Shame

The third category is guilt and shame. They go hand in hand. When we feel guilty, we feel shame. When we feel shame, we feel guilty. Guilt means we are "held in, bound by, liable to a charge or action at law."[5] Guilt relates to being brought under judgment. Shame is disgrace or dishonor, feeling filthy. Shame is also brought on someone as judgment.

We have experienced a lot in our lives—trauma at others' hands and trauma caused by our actions. The damage leaves open wounds in our spirits. Grief engulfs us.

As I write this book, I continue to pray for you as you walk through this journey to remove these toxins. I am convinced this process will free you from the guilt and shame you carry. You may try to create another wall, but through this continual practice, you will grow stronger.

If these issues are so deep you feel you cannot do this alone, seek counseling. Professionals can walk alongside you in a more in-depth process.

Shame and guilt lie to us. They tell us no one believes what we've been through. I believe you. I am with you. I know you can do this. And better yet, Jesus knows.

With guilt and shame come unforgiveness and sadness. Blame, resentment, and regret follow. These toxins can result from past experiences or current struggles.

The scripture from Colossians 3 lists some of the sins God directs us to get rid of: anger, rage, malice, slander, and filthy language.

I urge you to look at not only the sins committed against you but also the sins you've committed. The longer we live with the toxins of guilt and shame, the more we create anxiety, self-pity, self-doubt, and low self-esteem. It is hard to let go of these toxins, but if you do, God is ready to fill you with His peace.

What are you willing to give up, and how do you begin?

The process is 3UP, 3DOWN. In baseball, when three batters come to bat and all three are out after the at-bat, the terminology used is three up, three down. The detox process we will use is much the same.

First, we'll take three steps to identify the emotional toxins, then

---

[5] W. E. Vines, *Vine's Expository Dictionary of NT Words, s.v.* "guilty," https://www.studylight.org/dictionaries/eng/ved/g/guilty.html.

three steps to remove them. Using this method is one small step toward the peace God gives us when we open our minds and hearts.

3UP

- ✒ **Pray it up.** Ask the Lord to reveal the first toxin He wants to eliminate. Pray for protection through the process.

  Example Prayer: "Lord, I open my mind and heart to you. I thank you for all you have done in my life. I thank you that your Holy Spirit is alive in me. Father, please reveal to me what toxins I am allowing to build a wall between us. I want to grow to be more faithful and trusting of you. Show me what I need to remove in my life. Protect me, Lord, as I work to clear away what stands in the way of my growth."

- ✒ **Dig it up.** Read through the categories. Was there a toxin category that jumped out? Focus on that category. Then choose a specific toxin that applies to you.

- ✒ **Set it up.** Write the one toxin in a journal. Say it aloud as you do. Feel the feel as you focus on the toxin. Journal the feelings. What do you see? What makes your heart race? What memory do you have relating to the specific suffering?

3DOWN

- ✒ **Lay it down.** Offer your burden to Jesus. He says, "Cast your cares on the LORD and he will sustain you; he will never let the righteous be shaken" (Psalm 55:22). Pile your troubles on God's shoulders. He'll carry your load, and help you out. He wants you to give your burdens to Him. He can handle it.

- ✒ **Put it down.** What will I do? The action of conviction. Each time you have a feeling or concern or another emotional barrier arises once again, prioritize the list of things you will do. Take the thought captive. Pray. Surrender to the Lord. Give it to Him. Replace it with scripture. Take a step away to focus on the encouragement of His Word.

- ✒ **Close it down.** Take a deep breath and close your eyes (unless you need them open to read this). Repeat to yourself: "God, you are able. Lord, you have given me purpose. Jesus, you can do all things in and through me to glorify you. I know I can leave these emotional barriers and step into the peace and confidence you offer so freely." Close it. Leave it.

We can overcome spiritual jet lag. Identify the emotional barriers. Surrender them to the Lord. They can only be released by action. By choosing a step, you will grow.

Are you brave enough to take this step forward? You are. God knows you are.

Detox Challenge

- Always begin with prayer.
- Pull out your fun, inspirational journal you can use for the Detox Challenge.
- Begin the 3UP, 3DOWN process.
- Prayer: "Lord, continue to work in and through me. I release the emotional barriers to you. I am brave enough to take the first step into freedom. I want to live a spiritually healthy life with you. In Jesus's name, amen."

CHAPTER 8
Know the Voice

Questions fill my mind when I think God has spoken to me. Scripture tells us to listen for God's guidance, but how do we know if it's God's voice, our internal dialogue, or the multiple voices in the world? When we figure out the source, decisions can come quickly.

I quickly ran up the steps past the Open House sign onto the wide porch to escape the steady rain. I knocked on the large green door. An older woman opened the door and greeted me with a broad smile. "Are you looking for a big house?"

Shocked by her question, I searched for words. My silence didn't stop her sales pitch. "This is the house if you are looking for one with lots of room. How many children do you have?" She didn't wait for a response.

She led me into the large foyer complete with a center staircase. She pointed to the third riser on the wide steps. "My wedding portrait was taken here."

The ornate rail was stained dark, the spindles painted a bright white. The well-worn steps were a shade lighter than the rail.

My tour guide, also the Realtor, shared that she and her three sisters had been raised in the home. When she paused, I told her I was not in the market for a big house. I didn't tell her immediately, but the home was way out of our price range.

Our current home was a lovely place to raise our boys. David and I had decided to expand the small house when the tiny closets became too small for our older boys' shoes. The dead-end street was the perfect location for three rambunctious boys.

We loved our neighbors and our neighborhood, but I decided to look at houses near the school our boys attended, to make sure no other home was better than the one we owned.

The day I happened upon this house, I had not found a better option. The only reason I stopped at the yellow house—my favorite color—was curiosity. The price tag far exceeded any other in the neighborhood.

The house was grand, perfectly placed on a corner hillside lot. It stood like a queen on her throne. Beautiful, but not an option for our budget.

When I parked in front, I checked the ad, and realized the open house wouldn't begin for another thirty minutes. The boys were at home with our foster baby. I'd been gone for over two hours and needed to return home.

As the rain fell harder, I drove toward home. My cell phone rang. David was calling from Toronto, and the game was about to start. I pulled over and answered.

I shared with him that the day had been disappointing, but I felt certain the Lord wanted us to stay in the blue house on the dead end. I would start the renovation plans that week.

David asked where I was, and I told him about the big yellow house on the corner hill. He encouraged me to wait and see it. He had spoken to the boys, and the baby was sleeping. "That house may give you ideas to help our renovation decisions," he said.

Some quiet time in the car alone would be a sweet respite from my ordinarily busy days. Raising three boys, homeschooling one, and fostering newborn babies didn't leave much leisure time.

Thirty minutes in the car listening to the rain pelt the roof would be restful. I reclined my seat and adjusted my mirror to watch the front of the house. Time to relax.

I think we should include God in every decision, but I didn't pray before entering the house on the corner. The price was more than we could pay, and honestly, the house was more space than I wanted to clean.

But the homeowner didn't want to hear my excuses. As I toured the house, she asked again about children. I told her I had three boys. Her next question was the beginning of a pivotal moment. "No girls?" she asked.

"Well, a baby girl is living with us at the moment." I gave a quick explanation of our fostering experience. I told her how I'd prayed about fostering, and one thing after another confirmed God wanted us to do it.

The first confirmation that God had called David and me to be foster parents came when a man at church shared about his foster care and adoption—what a positive impact his foster and adoptive parents had on him. A few days later, I watched a news program documenting the need for foster parents and the lack of applicants in our area. Next, a phone call survey asked our opinion of the foster care system. I took these as answers to our prayers.

Tori was the first baby we had the honor of fostering. She arrived a few days after David and I became certified as foster parents. Born just before Christmas, she was a gift from the Lord to the world.

The foster care supervisor called at 9:00 a.m., December 26. I was at the store a few hours later, picking up diapers and wipes. I prayed without ceasing as I pushed the cart through the store. Thoughts and questions bombarded me:

Have we made the right decision? A scripture from the book of James came to mind.

"Suppose a brother or a sister is without clothes and daily food. If one of you says to them, 'Go in peace; keep warm and well fed,' but does nothing about their physical needs, what good is it? (James 2:15–16).

What will I do about cooking for the boys if I have a newborn with extra needs? A text arrived from a friend at our church: "We are bringing meals for this week."

God, I can't do this on my own. "We who are strong ought to bear with the failings of the weak and not to please ourselves" (Romans 15:1).

Fostering wasn't about me; it was an opportunity to serve Him. His Word gave me the understanding and wisdom I needed.

That day at the yellow house, the homeowner gave me the label of sainthood in the upstairs hallway. I told her I was obeying God, not doing it for selfish gain. Our conversation through the rest of the house was about obedience to God. Like my prayers about fostering, she too had prayed about selling her family home. The Lord told her He would bring the perfect family, one to whom she could comfortably pass the torch of her family home.

She proclaimed that we were that family. I disputed. I said several times that we were unable to meet her asking price. Embarrassed I was only looking because of my nosiness, I apologized profusely for wasting her time. She continued to pull me from room to room, up one staircase, then down another.

As the tour ended, she grabbed my hands and prayed out loud, asking the Lord to convince me this house was right for our family. She blessed the house as a place of ministry to others.

In my spirit, I felt the Lord say, *It shall be.*

"Make me an offer," she said.

I physically trembled as I climbed down the many steps in front of the house. I crossed the street and stood at my car as families walked by on their way to a nearby park.

David was in the middle of a game. I couldn't call him. I didn't want to share such a crazy story with the boys and get their hopes up. At that moment, the only person I could talk to about the house was God.

The following events happened quickly and were utterly more than I could have accomplished or imagined. David and I prayed for God's guidance. Great peace came over us even though we were nervous. We agreed to move forward.

A Realtor friend thought I was crazy to come in with such a low offer when the asking price was so much higher. But the homeowner and her family came together, approved, and accepted our offer. Our blue house on the dead end sold for more than we expected.

The yellow house on the hill became a home pleasing to God. We held Bible studies with atheists, teenagers, and mothers from the boys' school. Small groups gathered. We had baptisms in our hot tub. A teen from England came for a year to work with our church. We hosted prayer groups and social events often. And two more babies were cared for until a permanent home could be found.

We could have easily talked ourselves out of purchasing the yellow house. Financial concerns. Another move. Too much to clean. But in the end, we sought the Lord. We expected to hear from Him. Hearing His call, we found wisdom and understanding in His small whispers and confirmations.

My sheep listen to my voice; I know them, and they follow me. I give them eternal life, and they shall never perish; no one will snatch them out of my hand.

–John 10:27

Jesus is our good shepherd. He knows His sheep and protects us, saving us from present danger and eternal harm. While we do suffer on earth, Satan cannot endanger our souls. He cannot take away our eternal life with God.

Choosing to follow Jesus gives us everlasting safety. We are not eternally secure because we grip God, but because He grips us. He's got us. He's hanging onto you.

I grew up on a farm and am a country girl at heart. I was always amazed at how the animals knew my daddy's whistle or call. But not until I raised a sheep for my 4-H project did I experience that bond myself. Daisy, my sheep, heard my voice and came running.

Daddy called her but to no avail. She only listened to me. Blocking out the noise around them, sheep hear their herder's unique sound and only follow their instructions.

I want to be a sheep who only hears my shepherd's call.

Listening to Jesus is our connection to His ability to lead us. Hearing God becomes more natural as our relationship deepens. Our connection deepens when we terminate the toxins that go against the truth God desires for us to know.

As we work through the termination process, we open our mind and heart to hear the Lord's direction. When we receive His Word and treasure His knowledge, we absorb and apply the guidance He offers. Our spiritual ears become attentive to His wisdom, and our heart opens to understanding. They are hidden treasures we search out as we grow closer to Him.

Pay attention to the shepherd's voice. Ask Him to teach you His ways, lead you to truth. Delight in the Lord. Hearing His voice opens your mind and spirit to allow His Spirit to work in you. But you have to choose to welcome His presence. With His presence comes His voice.

At night sheep are often kept in a pen to protect them from thieves, weather, or wild animals. In the days of Jesus, sheep pens were caves, sheds, or open areas surrounded by walls made of stone or branches.

The shepherd often slept at the entrance of the enclosure to protect the sheep. The shepherd acted as a gate that protected them during the night, then led them out to a safe place to graze in the morning.

Jesus is our gate to God's salvation and safety. He leads and guides us to our purpose. He shepherds us because He loves us. He isn't just doing a job or leading us aimlessly. He is committed to loving us. He laid down His life for our salvation and eternal life with Him.

With our ears open, we seek His understanding and wisdom. The Bible tells us about the Israelites' hearts being far from God even though they professed Him with their words. Our hearts and our lips need to be in sync with the Lord's voice.

What's essential to help us hear? To hear doesn't take much effort. It is involuntary, accidental, and effortless. When a tree falls, we hear the crack when it breaks, the swoosh as it falls, and the thump when it hits the ground. We don't have to do anything. Hearing God's voice is similar. He talks to us, and we hear His words. But do we listen? Are there too many other noises drowning out His voice?

We cannot depend on our thoughts and emotions to steer us down the right path. We have to learn to discern the voice of God in all the other noise. Listen to your shepherd's voice. Become so aware of who God is that you can clearly detect what is from God and what is not. Muting the toxic voices enables us to hear His.

What's essential to help us listen? Listening is an intentional act. It requires focus and mandates the removal of all distractions such as fear, unbelief, and guilt. We have to be active readers of the Word so we can see God's signs and listen to His words.

God has created us for a close relationship with Him. Listening creates a feeling of respect, connection, and understanding, which improves our relationship with Jesus. Removing the emotional barricades creates more freedom for the Lord's whispers to be heard more clearly.

To master listening, we have to practice. Careful listening offers an opportunity to understand His call. Most of us don't listen to the Lord to understand His will but to create a scenario that fits our desires. Begin a practice to listen for His desires.

Our goal is to be spiritually mature. Hearing His voice is an act of maturity. Be assured He is willing to speak. He is already speaking. Receive and respond with thanksgiving.

God speaks to us in many ways: through His Word, the wind whispering in the treetops, or a scripture shared by a trusted friend. What is God saying to you?

The Lord communicates in different forms. Many of us will never hear the audible voice of God this side of heaven, but there are other ways we can hear Him.

How do we know the voice we hear is God and not our desires tainted by outside noise? We run it through the spiritual sound check.

Does what we're hearing align with scripture? We read the Bible for our scripture check. His Word is alive and active. With a disciplined practice of reading God's Word, we can learn more about Him and what He says.

When we read His Word, our ears are trained to hear His voice. Reading the Bible is a first step in connecting with Him more profoundly. But don't stop with a rote routine of reading. Sit quietly. Ask the Lord to speak to you. As you read the Word, who God is and what He says becomes easier to understand.

As we fall more and more in love with Jesus, we learn to listen. We can determine what lines up with scripture and what doesn't.

Exchanging emotional barriers with scripture increases our hearing. We hear His call because we know His voice. Effective listening comes with an open communication loop with Him through knowing scripture.

When we are focused on God's Word, scripture comes to mind, confirming His help. In our prayer time, we feel a sense of peace, warmth, and excitement. God is with us. He is ready to answer us—maybe not in the way we want, but He will answer according to His purpose and plan. Intentionally set aside time to listen to God.

I know the essence of the verses, maybe not the exact wording. When I begin to question God's voice, the words pop into my head. The words may not be in perfect order, but I know they are of God. The more we read His Word, the more it becomes part of our spiritual language.

Does what we've heard affirm God's character? Much like the voice lining up with scripture, we want to make sure what we hear aligns with who God is. In chapter five, we looked at examples of who God is and what He promises. Use God's character as a gauge.

If God is love, but what you hear is to say something hurtful to someone else, that is not God's voice. Are you feeling hatred toward an individual? That is not from God. If God is good, but you hear you are a failure, those words are not the voice of God.

Keep the list of God's character traits and what He promises close by for reference. Measure what you hear by His character.

Is what we are hearing beyond our capabilities? If we can do it on our own for our image or for others to notice, then we will probably rely on our voice and our power rather than the Lord's. Do we have to rely on His strength because ours is not sufficient?

If the answer we hear is based on what we already know how to accomplish without God's help, then we already have that under control. When God calls us into a space where we can only accomplish the task with His help, we are hearing His voice.

Is it pleasing to God? We always want to stay on the side of pleasing and glorifying God. We often find our place of comfort and safety in what we know and what makes us feel good. What pleases us is often our natural desire, safety, and comfort. But pleasing God is the safest place we can be.

God speaks to us every day. He invites us to draw close to Him and listen. Sometimes He whispers; other times His voice is loud and clear. Almost deafening.

Trying to hear from God can create frustration and confusion when we want an answer but don't seem to get it. Maybe we are asking the wrong question. Ask God what He is teaching you in the waiting. Don't get stuck in doubt and discouragement. Pause, pray, and pursue God. He is there, ready to guide and lead you.

Is it being confirmed? Dreams, thoughts, and prayer are three ways God speaks. Have there been times when you had to make a weighty decision, and you dreamed about how God would walk you through it? Are those thoughts lining up with God's Word? Are prayers giving great peace? Has a sermon spoken directly to you?

When God speaks, the words, the scripture, and the prayer align with what we've been debating. The movie you are watching may use the same language you have been praying when asking for direction.

A podcast topic may be so applicable that God seems to speak directly into your heart. That, my friend, is confirmation.

Do trusted friends agree the voice is God's? A spiritually mature person can guide you through prayer patterns and practices to help deepen and broaden your walk with God. Becoming part of a prayer group is one way to practice the prayer disciplines.

When you feel lonely and isolated, reach out to someone you admire and trust. It may be someone at church, in a Bible study group, or a friend from the past. Older or younger. Different economic standing. Different race. Different culture. Stretch your inner circle to include many types of people. Include others in the group if you want to enlarge it. I suggest pairing up into accountability partners when the circle grows.

Begin your time with prayer. Invite the Holy Spirit to be part of your time together. Even if it is only two of you, start with prayer.

If the group is larger, encourage a different person to pray each time. Encourage one another to listen to the Lord. Help others discern God's call. There's no right way to pray. Be as authentic and honest with the Lord as you would want your child to be with you. Prayer is a conversation with Jesus. Listen for His response.

Groups have gathered in my home, on rooftop terraces in cities, at picnic tables at a ballpark, and online. No one way or place is any better than another. Anytime you take time is the best time. Take time for one another, help each person in the group to hear God's voice. With each desire for guidance, pause and listen for God's guidance. You can and will hear Him when you listen.

Listen for God's voice in everything you do, everywhere you go. He's the one who will keep you on track. Don't assume you know it all. Run to Him.

Know His voice. Hear His call.

Detox Challenge

- Always begin with prayer.
- Pull out your fun, inspirational journal you use for the Detox Challenge.
- Get a sparkly pen.
- Write the decision, desire, question, or need you want God to speak about in your life. It can be more than one.
- If there is more than one, leave room underneath to put what you hear through the Spiritual Sound Check.
- The Spiritual Sound Check
  - Does it align with scripture?
  - Does it affirm God's character?
  - Is it beyond your capabilities?
  - Is it pleasing to God?
  - Is it being confirmed in sermons, dreams, or your quiet time with God?
  - Do trusted friends agree the voice is God's?
- Pause.
- Listen.
- Hear His voice.

CHAPTER 9
Called Confidence

My personality presents as self-confident, strong, and assertive. God created me to be a force of nature, for Him. I never want to step out of place when it comes to what He has created me to be or what He has called me to do. I work every day to honor and glorify the Lord, not other people, and strive to fulfill my purpose as a Christian.

Over the years, lack of confidence isn't something I dealt with much. More people told me I was overconfident. Too bold for a lady. Too joyful and loud. As a kid, I was confident in who God made me, and I lived life to the fullest.

When I felt the Lord calling me to write, I was sure God would accomplish it if He called me to it. Writing wasn't something I could achieve on my own, but I could be successful with the His guidance.

A book contract came in less than two years, followed by advice from many sources about what I needed to do to keep writing. The recommendations seemed overwhelming.

I began working on my writing skills, serving my readers, building a following on social media—everything I was supposed to do based on guidance from other authors. I worked and worked, submitted ideas, book proposals, and my heart along with them. Rejections came one after another. Keep writing, they said.

I felt incapable of doing what was necessary to pursue a writing career. I found no purpose, no value. I focused on failure, lack of knowledge, and what I didn't accomplish. I based my value and worth on the rejections, losing my focus on why I was writing. Self-focus took my eyes off of what God desired.

I decided I couldn't continue writing, so I set that dream aside. Before I tackled writing, my dream was to become a speaker. For quite a few years, I had spoken to small groups, mostly baseball wives, so I signed up for a speaker conference.

Remember loud and talkative? That was my comfort zone. I love being with people, hearing their stories, and giving hugs—so unlike the solitary life of writing.

At the speaker's conference, the director asked me how things were going. I shared my struggles with writing and my pivot to speaking. She asked some great questions and affirmed me as an author. I had a published book two years earlier, earning me the title.

Then she asked a profound question, "Have you been writing as a hobby or a career?"

I didn't have a clear answer.

She encouraged me to take a step back and evaluate my view of writing.

I pondered the hobby or career question for a while after that conference. Writing was such a new concept that I didn't take my abilities, God's gifts, seriously. Writing was something smart readers who always dreamed of publishing embraced as a career—not girls like me, who didn't read an entire book in high school and had been told in elementary school that I wasn't a good reader. Another teacher in high school said I didn't understand what I was reading. I devalued my intellect because of others' opinions.

I was always a math and science girl, not a literary scholar. I loved numbers and experiments. I studied nursing in college and worked as an ICU nurse. I didn't think I was qualified to be a writer.

However, I couldn't say writing was a hobby because I grew to love words. I learned to enjoy reading as an adult. New words invigorate me; books inspire me. I challenge myself to learn better writing techniques and grow every day. I read for pleasure and to learn.

Could I live somewhere in the middle of a hobby and a career? The emotional toxins I believed I had left behind told me no. I focused on how I didn't measure up. I couldn't see myself the way God saw me. I didn't accept what He saw, only what the toxins said.

- You are a fraud.
- Not enough.
- Too much.
- Not smart.
- You have nothing to say anyone wants to read.
- You don't belong in the same room as other writers, authors.

My confidence was missing in action. Taking the thoughts captive, I rebutted them with facts. I am an author with a published book. The words the Lord gives me matter. One person who read my first book said, "Your book changed my life. The Lord speaks to me every day. He is working in me and through me. Relationships are being healed. Thank you for listening to the Lord and writing this book."

I searched my Bible for the scripture I relied on early in my call to write. I made small notecards with the concept of that scripture and others, replacing the toxins in my thoughts.

- Write the vision, make it understandable, so those who read it may run with it.
- Encourage others with sound teaching.
- God has a plan for my life.
- He directs me and guides me.

My friend's words and the scriptures were a balm to my soul. Why did I start writing? To obey the Lord. That's the easy answer, but there was something more. I wanted to help Christian women overcome the obstacles that kept them far from God. Helping my friends deepen their relationship with Christ, allowing Him to work in their lives, is my greatest honor.

Helping others wasn't in my abilities or my value. It was in the value of Christ. He gave me gifts to use, and I had snuffed out the fire He placed inside me. I left the gifts He gave me in a box in the corner. I gave them no place in my life. I didn't value who He said I was.

Holding fast to the message from the Lord, I believed and received the qualification He had given me to encourage others with sound teaching.

I decided to accept the calling the Lord has placed on my life, the purpose God had given me in this world, the joy and exuberance He gifted to me. God has a plan for my life, and I will do everything I can to fulfill all that He desires to do.

Through different circumstances over time, I lost my confidence when I focused on my shortcomings. The detox helped me see God trusted me, and new opportunities presented themselves. It was time to release myself and God. It takes courage to have confidence.

I pondered some hard questions.

- Could I hope in God?
- Do I have more confidence in God than in my negative thoughts and shortcomings?
- Is my belief in His abilities greater than my desire to grip what I can in my hands?
- Am I confident in Him?

I had believed the lies and devalued God and myself. I became discouraged when I kept trying but still felt inadequate and unqualified. People's voices were louder than God's.

We build confidence not by relying on our ability but by trusting God. Knowing God's voice, I listened.

Because of who God is and who He has created me to be, I dedicated my life to His message. I had to deny myself and increase Jesus to find peace and freedom. I have confidence that I can approach God with all requests and trust in Him for all things.

He said to her, "Daughter, your faith has healed you. Go in peace and be freed from your suffering."

–Mark 5:34

Jesus knew power had gone out from Him. He was in the middle of a large crowd. They were pressing in around Him.

"Who touched my clothes?" He asked.

The disciples must have chuckled. After all, it was a great crowd. Many were near Jesus and bumping Him. But Jesus recognized the difference between someone bumping into Him and someone touching Him in faith. The touch of desperate faith connected to His kingdom power. He couldn't ignore it. He knew who had touched Him, but He wanted her to step forward.

The woman in the crowd that day had struggled for twelve years with a seemingly incurable condition, which caused her to bleed continuously. The medical condition was a significant hindrance and made her ritually unclean and excluded her from social interaction. The burden of separation must have laid heavy on her heart. She had nothing left. If defined only by her circumstances, she was desperate, suffering, needy, poor, and afraid. Others probably devalued her because of her condition. She may have even devalued herself.

But she wasn't hopeless. She had a sliver of hope. A mustard seed of faith. She was courageous and bold because she hoped in God. She wasn't a committed follower with deep devotion, but she'd heard of Jesus's works and believed He could heal her. She was so desperate to be healed she risked making Jesus unclean by touching Him.

When she touched His cloak, Jesus's healing went straight from His body to her body, to her identity. There is a difference between curious and timid people and those who courageously reach out and touch Him. She believed the touch of His cloak was enough to heal her because she focused on what He could do in her life.

She came forward, fell at His feet, and worshipped Him, confessing what she'd done. Jesus said, "*Daughter*, your faith has healed you." My emphasis is on *daughter*. I want you to feel His inclusion, His love toward her and us. Her identity. Jesus accepted and loved her as His daughter. She was valuable to Him. He called her daughter because she was His child. No questioning if she was qualified, good, smart, or powerful enough. With confidence in who He was, she boldly stepped through that crowd to gain access to His authority.

All people need to know they matter. They want to know they matter to someone and they are valuable.

- **We are enough.**
- **We matter.**
- **We are valuable.**

Simply because we are His daughters we are valued. If we as parents love our children so deeply, just imagine how much the Creator of the universe loves us.

Merriam-Webster defines *confidence* as full of conviction, certain. *Self-confidence* is having or showing assurance and self-reliance. As the daughters of Christ, our confidence is having or showing assurance in His power and relying on Him.

Our confidence comes from Him, not us. Our faith gives us boldness to step out in faith as a daughter of Christ. He strengthens us. Giving our thoughts or others' opinions more influence in our lives than God separates us from His strength.

His Spirit fills us with power. We have access and authority because He lives inside us. He doesn't instruct us to have self-confidence but to have courage—confidence in Him.

God calls us His daughter, inviting us into a new beginning with a unique purpose. He finds great value in us. We don't have to feel wholly equipped. God will provide what we need to accomplish what He calls us to do. Confidence comes from Jesus—in who He is and who He created us to be in and with Him.

We are the daughters of the King. He has spoken over our lives. Reach out to Him. Faith healed the woman because she believed that if she touched His garment she would be healed. Denying herself, she relied on His power. Jesus says we only need a mustard seed of faith to move a mountain (Matthew 17:20).

I want us to be fearless like Daniel when he was in the lion's den. Hope like Moses in the wilderness. Be bold like David with that stone and slingshot. We can do anything God calls us to do when have faith and courage. The will of God will not take us where He will not protect us.

Jesus did not say He healed her. Her faith healed her. Jesus told her, "Go in peace and be freed." With a touch of His robe, she was healed and filled with peace and freedom.

We're learning to hear the Lord's voice. Now we must choose to believe and hope in Him. Take thoughts captive when they present themselves. Release them to the Lord. Replace them with scripture. Feel the feelings but let go of what is not redeeming and life-giving.

Trusting God takes practice. We have to choose to do it every day.

How do we live in that place of faith and hope that heals, empowers, and give us courage? Remember who God is and what He promises, the source of peace and freedom.

In chapter 5, we learned who God is and what He promises. God is our protector, rescuer, and comforter. He loves us more than we can imagine and protects us from enemies. He rescues us from ourselves and comforts us when we are hurting. Continuing to grow in believing, now we look at who He's created us to be as His daughters.

We are called children of God. When we receive the Lord as our Savior, we have the right to be called children of God (Romans 8:14). He created our innermost being. Before He formed us in our mother's womb, He knew us (Psalm 139:15–16). No matter the circumstance of conception or birth, we are fearfully and wonderfully made by the creator of the earth. What great love the Father has extended to us!

We are children of God no matter how we feel or what we think. We are His children based on scripture, not the narrative that runs in our minds. We are who the great I Am says we are. We may be works in progress, but we are His children.

Jesus trusts us as His daughters. We are kept in perfect peace when our minds are centered on Him. He depends on you to use the unique gifts He's given you.

He gives us authority to use the gifts He provides to honor and glorify Him. Think about that. God trusts us. Are we responsible? Authentic, dependable, and honorable for the kingdom? God desires us to rely on Him and the promises of His word.

If God trusts us, how can we ever doubt His ability to transform us? How can we lack confidence in Him?

Trusting Him coincides with His trust in us. Believing in the "immeasurably more" that He desires to do is the foundation of confidence. He has created us as His daughters—daughters of the King.

This does not give you a mantle to hold over the world, forcing your way through life. It is a torch you carry to shine the light of Christ. Our responsibility is to represent Jesus in all we do, say, and are. We are accountable for presenting Christ to others.

As His daughters, we are new creations. When we gave our lives to Christ and committed to following Him, our past was wiped away. We are forgiven and accepted. We have a clean slate. Pure. We are Jesus's creation. We are created to live our life for God's glory.

The old has passed away; the new has come (1 Corinthians 5:17). We no longer have to yield to sin. God protects us from the evil around us because we are His new creation. We live with the seed of God inside of us. Ready to grow. Abiding in the Word of God. Renewed because we are created in His image.

When we think of being made in the image of God, we cannot condemn ourselves. If we do, then we condemn Him. Our past has no hold on us. Our future holds His promises, peace, and freedom.

Being daughters of God means we are completely loved. God is love. No matter how much we mess up, doubt, or struggle, God loves us. He created us as He desired. He loves us unconditionally, and nothing will ever change that fact.

God loves us so much that He sent His Son to take the burden of our sins. In Christ's death, we are forgiven. We now live out that love because He first loved us. His love manifests in joy, peace, patience, kindness, goodness, faithfulness, gentleness, and self-control.

As daughters, we have a responsibility to shine His light into a dark world. We are a vessel to share Jesus with the world. Our identity in Christ gives us confidence and peace. It gives us purpose and a calling. We cannot sit back and do nothing. Being God's daughters empowers us to utilize the incredible power He places in us with His Holy Spirit.

We have been given the power to overcome all emotional toxins. Satan desires to overwhelm our spirits, to smother God's light. In God, we have courageous confidence.

Confidence is not the same thing as courage. It cannot exist without courage. Courage cannot be mustered up on our own. Confidence may make it easier to have courage, but it cannot be manufactured.

Courage is attained from faith, from believing in God's Word, power, character, and promises. Faith manifests courage. Courageous faith believes that all things are possible with God.

Courageous confidence is living with the peace and freedom God gives us when we are confident of who He is, who He has created us to be, and the purpose and calling He has for us. Living a life of courage is a torch worthy to carry.

The lessons we learn from the detox are what we rely on for peace and freedom. Satan wants to take the mighty gifts God has given us and replace them with all the emotional toxins we've gripped way too long. Having the confidence to flee from Satan and seek the love of Christ comes as we detox from the tethered toxins.

We train our mind to be stronger than Satan's schemes. Focus on knowing what to ignore. Fix our eyes on what to believe. Hold fast to the faithful message God has given us. We are qualified to share in the inheritance of the kingdom, encourage others, and respond to naysayers.

Our name is Daughter. We have more than a mustard seed of faith ready to grow inside of us. We can choose to make Him our one and only, our refuge and fortress.

You, my friend, can approach Jesus with confidence. You are valuable to Him. Find your courage and boldness in Jesus. Your name, Daughter, confirms Jesus's confidence in you and empowers your courageous confidence. Believe Him. Be free and full of peace.

We can do this together. One step at a time.

Are you ready to experience the extraordinary future God has for you? Get that crown ready. Make sure you have some strong bobby pins to hold it in place. We're going on an adventure with courageous confidence.

Detox Challenge

- Always begin with prayer.
- Pull out that fun, inspirational journal you use for the Detox Challenge.
- Get a sparkly pen.
- Are there feelings or thoughts you need to continue to put through the 3UP, 3DOWN assignment?
- Pause.
- Listen.
- Hear His voice.
- He calls you Daughter. Write in your journal the three statements that define what being a daughter of God means.
    - I am enough.
    - I matter.
    - I am valuable.
- Replace *I* or *me* with your name in the following statements: I am a child of God; He trusts me; I am a new creation; I am completely loved. Examples:
    - Pam is a child of God.
    - He trusts Susan.
    - Debi is a new creation.
    - Jessica is completely loved.
- Write these statements.
    - I have confidence in the Lord.
    - He trusts me.
    - I am enough.
    - I am worthy.
    - I am free.
    - I have peace.
    - I have courageous confidence.
- Who is one friend or acquaintance God is calling you to build up in courageous confidence? Pray for that person. Get in touch with her. Invite her to join you in the journey.

CHAPTER 10
One Day at a Time

The first night of our annual Christian baseball conference, The Increase, I felt a nudge in my spirit. The worship band was playing. I don't remember the song. My hands held high, I prayed. I had allowed the emotional toxins to get me stuck in doubt and discouragement. I was hiding from God and what He asked me to do. I heard God but did not listen.

That night I asked Him to release me because I was ready for whatever He had in mind. I knew I had been asking for the wrong things before.

I prayed again. *Lord, I'm ready. I submit to you and our desires. I've hidden from you for far too long. I'm ready to step out of my comfort zone into the brave. I trust you, Lord, even if I don't know what the plan is.*

Let's go! I heard and felt deep in my spirit.

Tears poured. I didn't have a step-by-step plan. My schedule was full of commitments, my brother's cancer was not better, and my mother's health was poor. David had lost his job, and we didn't know what lay ahead. I didn't feel ready, but God called me to go.

Many times I've had great desires to do more. Be more. Make more of an impact. But with three young boys and a husband who was away from home eight months a year, I felt stuck.

I often created a plan to do something I found valuable. Put in a splash of prayer and a pinch of trust in the Lord and ran. My arrogant assumption that I could accomplish it overran my belief that I needed God every step of the way.

Oh, how I love to run ahead with my well-laid-out plan. My plan, not His. I included Jesus in my list. I searched for the scripture that fit what I wanted. I prayed for it all to come together and fall into place. I made a three-to-five-year goal, then I bulldozed my way through life, trying to accomplish it.

So many things went wrong. I stepped on the wrong toes trying to get my way. I grew angry with my children needing me when I wanted to complete a task. I ignored David's phone calls because my checklist loomed in front of me. Then I asked, "Where are you, Lord?"

My long-term goals were worthy. I wanted to raise money for a charity. Create a girls' club for underprivileged girls. Write a curriculum for a women's center that helped women with healthcare, self-care, and baby care.

I desired to spend time in the mission field with children who needed Jesus, food, and shoes. I wanted to make a difference in the world. World peace. You know, the small stuff.

I put too much emphasis on my calling, on God's great plan for my life. I forgot to listen to what He had already called me to do. I had too many directives of my own to understand and achieve what God desired.

I spent too much time worrying about my call, impact, and desires. I focused on my list, not God's guidance. I wanted purpose and meaning, but only if it fit into what I viewed as successful.

The divine force over my life was there, but I wasn't allowing God to direct my steps. When I slowed my thoughts and checked off tasks, I heard the Lord loud and clear but then questioned if it was God's voice.

After the conference, I laid out my goals and objectives. I created a master plan of what I wanted to accomplish for my ministry. My yearly goals were lofty but attainable. I set smaller goals for each month, then broke them down into daily steps toward accomplishing the end goal.

I prayed for success and advancement—"Please, Lord, help me get where I need to go." Each week I reviewed my objectives, but many outcomes weren't what I planned. I checked steps off of my list, but they took me in a different direction than I thought they would.

My biggest failures were those plans and desires that I allowed Jesus into rather than following His plan that He'd called me to join. I thought I knew where I was going. I had a definite method of accomplishing my goals, but that didn't always work out.

Finding my identity in the accomplishments kept me stagnant and limited my opportunities to serve as God desired. I was pushing through with selfish ambition and hindering His commission. I overlooked God's evident will as I stormed through the obstacles. When plans went wrong, I became terrified and shut down, redirected, or repurposed my aspirations.

During the detox of emotional barriers, the realization hit me. My plans failed not because I heard the wrong directive—I had heard *Go!*—but because I headed in the wrong direction.

The day David and I met, he said he knew he had to begin carrying a parachute at all times. He never knew what adventure I would pull him into next. I had put that parachute away because of all of my emotional toxins. Time to pull it out. I was parachute-ready.

The master plan was my mental trajectory. When I allowed God to direct my steps, He gave me direction to move forward even if I didn't know all the steps, even if I didn't see the big plan in front of me.

Through the detox, I learned to hear and trust. Now it was time to go. I took it one day at a time. Go and then He'll show.

On my wall, I've hung a quote from John Henry Newman, an English theologian, and poet.

> God has created me to do Him some definite service; He has committed some work to me which He has not committed to another. I have my mission—I never may know it in this life, but I shall be told it in the next. . . . I am a link in a chain, a bond of connexion between persons. He has not created me for naught. I shall do good, I shall do His work; I shall be an angel of peace, a preacher of truth in my own place, while not intending it, if I do but keep His commandments and serve Him in my calling.

> Therefore I will trust Him. Whatever, wherever I am, I can never be thrown away. If I am in sickness, my sickness may serve Him; in perplexity, my perplexity may serve Him; if I am in sorrow, my sorrow may serve Him.[6]

God has given us some definite service. He has committed work to us, a unique position. Newman's quote guides me to turn back to the meaning and purpose of my life in serving Jesus. My calling.

That day when evening came, he said to his disciples,
"Let us go over to the other side."

–Mark 4:35

He called them to go. They left the crowd and their stressful day behind. Jesus told them to get into the boat and go to the other side. Other boats went along with them. The disciples trusted the Lord's direction enough to go with Him to a destination He determined. The other side.

God promises to take us to the other side when He calls us to go with Him. The disciples lived daily in the presence of Jesus. Sometimes, we can be jealous of that position. Most of us would love to be face-to-face with Jesus here on earth, following His direction each day.

Then we step past our envy and realize we are in His presence every day. We've learned to overcome the emotional toxins and open

---

[6] John Henry Newman, *Part III, Meditations on Christian Doctrine with a Visit to the Blessed Sacrament Before Meditation,* March 7, para 2-3. From the Newman Reader—Works of John Henry Newman, The National Institute for Newman Studies. https://www.newmanreader.org/works/meditations/meditations9.html.

up to God's presence through the detox. The promise He gives us to protect, guide, and lead us to the other side is rooted in His Spirit in us.

He invites us, according to our ability, to listen to His Holy Spirit. He has gifted us with spiritual gifts He can tap into at any time. He calls us to go.

God calls us. We do not call ourselves. Our calling is not in the future tense. Jesus asks us to get in the boat and go to the other side. The disciples trusted Jesus, boarded the boat, and began their journey. They didn't know what was on the other side. Nor were they privy to the happenings along the way. No defined plan and outcome were discussed. They relied on their faith in who Jesus was and who they were as His followers.

The Sea of Galilee lies nearly seven hundred feet below sea level, surrounded by mountains and highlands. Because of its geography, the area is predisposed to violent windstorms.

As Jesus and the disciples crossed, a fierce gale blew. Not only were the disciples being tossed around, but the waves were also breaking over the boat. Several disciples were lifelong, professional fishermen. They had sailed through many storms. But in this "furious squall," they were terrified the boat would sink (Mark 4:37–38).

The disciples were in the center of God's will. They had followed Jesus's call to go with Him on the boat.

Even when we obey, life can grow stormy. Jesus doesn't promise smooth sailing. When we're caught in a storm while in the will of God, we may be doing what God tells us to do, but it still rains.

Even in Jesus's presence, the disciples doubted. While they relied on their thoughts and feelings, they were terrified. Their thoughts had filled them with doubt.

Where was Jesus during the storm? In the boat on a cushion, asleep. He hadn't just fallen asleep where He was sitting. Jesus curled up on a cushion and got comfortable. He was intentional.

When our problem overrides His promise, we doubt. When His plan is not laid out in detail, we grow discouraged. God doesn't want circumstances to outshine His Word or His presence. Remember,

He promised the "other side." We have to restructure our priorities.

The disciples doubted and questioned but woke Jesus up. They knew He would have an answer. His humanity was asleep, but His deity was awake. Jesus was not ignoring the situation. He was aware.

"Where are you, God?" we cry. As if He isn't there. Like He's sleeping on our call, plan, and purpose. But in the boat with the disciples, Jesus was just chilling. He knew they were okay. He knows. He has a plan.

Don't be scared of the wrong thing. Jesus's humanity feels. His deity fixes. Commit to living out His plan one day at a time.

The disciples were not thinking about the Lord being in their midst. They were terrified because of their external circumstances. Then they scared themselves even more, creating internal turmoil. Terror led to doubt. They woke Him and asked, "Teacher, don't you care if we drown?" (Mark 4:38).

Jesus got up, rebuked the wind, and calmed the sea. He spoke to the storm first. Jesus is God. He is Sovereign. The creation obeyed its creator. He then turned to the disciples and asked, "Do you still have no faith?" He spoke to the external circumstance before turning to the disciples and their internal turmoil. Both responded to His authority.

The disciples shook in awe of the wind and waves obeying this man. Jesus called them to go to the other side. In the journey, a storm terrified them. They doubted. Jesus showed up powerfully in spite of their unbelief. He had told them they would make it to their destination.

Our faith fails when we question our call. Trust that Jesus will take us to the other side.

Godly ambition should be our goal—serving the Lord and living as faithful servants. Our selfish ambition, our jobs, or our status often become our basis of meaning and purpose. We get lost in the desire to know all the details and control the steps leading to an outcome.

According to *Merriam-Webster*, a calling is a strong inner impulse toward a particular course of action, especially when accompanied by conviction of divine influence. The definition we often cling to is the vocation or profession which we choose. We confuse calling with career. We believe success in our profession and status is who we are. But the job is not our calling; our position is not the source of our identity. We find our calling and identity in Jesus.

When the Lord is our source for what matters and what it means, we find what He desires us to do. He provides.

Don't worry about tomorrow. Today has enough worries of its own. God cares so much that He gives us what we need to achieve what He has called us to do. God provides.

We begin with courageous confidence, trusting in God's plan. It is our responsibility to continue to seek Him and to follow His direction one day at a time.

As Christians, we have three types of calling. First, the Call of All. We are all called to believe in Jesus, turn away from sin, turn toward God, and glorify Him in all we say, do, and are. We are called to be obedient. We submit to God's plan and hope for our future. He does nothing in vain. He knows what He is about.

We are made in His image. As image bearers, we reflect the likeness of Christ—first to our families then to the world. We reflect the image of God in the way we live, speak, and serve. Jesus in skin. Called to be His vessels and to shine His light.

Next, the Internal Call beckons us to draw closer to the Holy Spirit, trusting in what God desires and listening to His whispers as He transforms us.

As believers, we are to live out what we know about who Christ is and who He has created us to be. We are to be a light to the world. Our lives should reflect the fruit of our Christian faith. We demonstrate the gifts of who we are created to be: love, joy, peace, patience, kindness, goodness, faithfulness, gentleness, and self-control.

The third is the Call to Go. Where do we feel Jesus pulling us? It may seem strange, different than anything you ever thought of or planned. His command to go is His desire to draw us into acts of service.

When the Lord tells us to go, He may not have revealed all that He has planned. He may not even shine a light on the first step. We begin by being obedient to the call. He may throw us among strangers, put us in an unfamiliar city, or the middle of nowhere. Or He may leave us right where we are but redirect our actions, direction, thoughts, or purpose.

Storms may arise. Even when we don't know the destination, we need to be obedient to His will, not ours. God is always with us. Stay focused on Him.

The three calling categories are interrelated. One depends on the other. Over time our Call to Go may be different, but our Call of All stays constant. Our Internal Call and Call to Go are carried out one day at a time. Each day we grow our Internal Call by drawing closer to Jesus.

- Pray to trust.
- Listen to hear.
- Step to go.
- One day at a time.

God created the heavens and the earth. He spoke, and there was light. God saw that it was good. He separated the light from the dark the first day. On the second day, God spoke and divided the waters from the heavens. Again, He spoke, and the land was created. Water was named ocean; the earth grew vegetation. The third day.

The fourth day, He spoke light in the skies, marking heaven and creating seasons. Then the fifth day, He spoke life to fish and other sea creatures, birds of all kinds. God spoke again, creating more living creatures on earth.

God spoke and created man in His image, reflecting the Trinity's nature. He gave man dominion over all the earth and living creatures. He saw all that He had made. The sixth day.

On the seventh, He rested. He had finished creation, and He rested from all His work. He made the day of rest holy.

One day at a time. If this pattern is good enough for God, it is good enough for us.

Start today. Begin to rewrite the plan believing that God promises the other side. When the Lord gives a directive, He gives direction. Trust that He will take you there. Find peace in His intention, even when you don't know what that is.

Having a spiritual health plan gives us guidance to rely first on Jesus. A list. My favorite thing. Create a list as a reminder to finish the detox with a healthy forward plan of action to follow Jesus.

We've learned to detox from the toxins as they arise to keep us clear of spiritual jet lag. We've also embraced the understanding of taking our thoughts captive, replacing them with scripture, and allowing the feelings but not getting stuck in them.

Hearing the Lord and listening to His voice helps us discern His direction and gain courageous confidence to act. Now we take our first steps toward where God is calling us.

The spiritual health plan we create will outline a plan of God's next best steps for our lives. We will take it one day at a time while Jesus pulls us forward.

The Health Plan's first step is writing three statements that I believe are true about you, and you should and will think about yourself.

- I am braver than I believe.
- I am smarter than I think.
- I am stronger than I seem.

The great I Am will take you to the other side.

The burning desire to live for something more significant has been put there by a big God. The yearning points us to Christ and to glorify Him as we take one next step.

Think about what fills you with passion. What are the things you do well? What do you love to do? Are there some things you do over and over without thinking much about them? Did God put those skills in you? Did He place that passion in your heart? Can you allow those skills to be used for God?

Write in the fun, inspirational notebook the one thing you desire to do for the Lord. Ask Him to show you how to have an impact: the big and the small. When you give yourself the freedom to dream, the Lord will show you what He desires.

Search the Bible to find verses that set your spirit on fire. Ask the Lord to reveal the passion and scripture.

- Terror may rise.
- Questions will increase.
- Doubt and discouragement will want to overtake.
- Remember what we've learned.
- Don't give up.

You don't have to be ready. Do it scared. Knees trembling, wake Jesus. He is prepared to speak to the storm and to you.

God created us with dreams to teach us our daily need for Him. Our lives are about Him. They allow us to serve Him and others and to glorify Him through it all.

Write a dream God has given you, the passion He has placed in your heart, in the journal. A God-sized plan to do some definite service for Him, one that only He can fulfill. The one that scares you, but you heard from Him. God-sized dreams refine us. They reveal to us that He is God and we are His. He promises the other side. Trust Him.

Write the scripture He showed you. Do you need to search for a few more to help you be courageous, brave, and bold? Do it. Write them down under your dream.

Listen for the God-given directive that gives you direction.

Is your parachute ready?

Dream so big only God can fulfill it. Start today. Rely on Jesus. Hear the call, listen, and go. One day at a time.

Detox Challenge

- Always begin with prayer.
- Pull out that fun, inspirational journal you use for the Detox Challenge.
- Get a sparkly pen.
- Jesus did it one day at a time. Use His plan.
- Spiritual Health Plan for today.
    - Go to your quiet space if you can.
    - Pray.
    - Read God's Word. Pull out your Bible, Bible app, or an audio version you can listen to if you're on the go.
    - Hear His voice in the scripture.
    - Ask Him to reveal your passion.
    - Listen to His guidance.
    - Choose a scripture that relates to your passion.
    - Take the first step of faith. Jesus will take you to the other side.
    - Start today and take it one day at a time.

CHAPTER 11

Change Her Story, Change History

In our distraction detox, we've removed toxic emotional barriers and learned how to recognize the destructive thoughts, take them captive, and replace them. As we move through the detox of removal, it's time to add the good. Impact lives for the kingdom of God.

For many years, I wanted to work in the mission field. When I was in high school, my dream was to become a nurse, join the Navy, travel the world, and do mission work in every country I visited.

I wanted to serve poor children in need, but that's not how my dream played out. God had a different path for me.

I met David while I was in college. Marriage wasn't on my agenda. God knew better. David and I had our first son in our second year of marriage. We added two more sons, losing three pregnancies along the way. Not the trajectory I had planned.

David's job took us many places. We lived in fifteen cities and towns in the US, Venezuela, and the Dominican Republic. Serving in our backyard took on a new meaning while we tried to survive day by day.

My dream was to serve abroad as a missionary. My view of being a missionary included a foreign country and children who needed food, medical attention, shoes, and Jesus. That kind of work involved more than a day trip. It required an extended stay. Don't ask me where I got this linear view of what serving God looked like, but it was my definition.

While experiencing the chaotic life of traveling for David's job, I grieved my inability to go on a foreign mission trip. Over the years, I signed up for trips with different groups or churches. Either the trips got canceled or our family's schedule changed. One opportunity after another fell through. Three little boys and a husband who traveled eight months a year didn't align with long-term service.

My desire to serve didn't stop because I couldn't pack up my life and go abroad. I longed to make a difference. I had a big-picture dream and wanted it fulfilled. I couldn't see what God had already placed in front of me, that the value of what He provided in the not-so-great appointments was as great as my overseas mission vision.

My skewed vision caused spiritual jet lag. I had a vision of my life story. Of how life was supposed to go and how God would create it for me. I had to move past my stagnant view and move into alignment with God's next steps.

As I let go of my grief over not getting what I wanted, I surrendered to the Lord. He then called me to go.

"So where do you want me to go?"

His response resonated deeply in my spirit. *Serve.*

"Well, Lord, I want to serve . . . children in a foreign country who need . . ."

I had to stop the repeated yearning for something I couldn't do. Break down the barricades. Change the script from what I wanted to what God wanted.

"Lord, show me where you want me to serve. Help me see who you want me to serve." *Go away to a secret place.*

A glimmer of hope.

"Ha! I cannot even use the bathroom without a son in there with me." Again, I had to stop the thoughts. "Lord, show me."

Immediately, I realized the Lord didn't want me physically to find a secret place but to allow Him access to the areas in my soul where I had not permitted Him.

I took out pen and paper and began to journal. I picked up my Bible and read it aloud, even when I wasn't alone. We listened to *Adventures in Odyssey* in the car as we drove from one baseball practice to another. The lessons touched my heart in a new way.

One night, I journaled, "Lord, you wanted me to go to a secret place. I know this is where you reside in me. I have served you by taking care of my spiritual life. Thank you, Lord, for this time."

Jesus had sent me to a place of serving Him by taking care of myself. It's hard to tell you I achieved any self-care. Women aren't good at it, at least I'm not. We definitely don't want to share with others that we practice self-care. What will they think? *Is she that selfish? She shouldn't be self-focused.*

We cannot serve others until we serve the one first. One God and one self. The distraction detox is one way to take care of ourselves. Build a strong foundation. We don't stop and only take care of ourselves. The foundation of being full of the Lord is necessary so the overflow pours out to others, to the one person God sends us to serve.

Time invested in pouring into my spiritual growth proved my need to stay connected with Jesus. Out of the overflow of His Spirit in me, I began to see the impact one life can have on one other life. I still had the big dream of serving overseas, but I saw the one life in front of me more clearly.

It started with me, then it grew to include another woman. Was it a woman I dreamed of spending time with? No. It was a sandpaper girl— the kind of person who rubs against the grain. The one I don't want to spend extra time with, who doesn't need anything because she has it all.

Little by little, I became more aware of the small ways I could serve where I was and who God put in front of me. In each city we lived in. The Dominican Republic. Ballparks and airports. For five minutes or a few months.

After I wrote my first book, our Baseball Chapel leader asked if I wanted to go on a mission trip with her. I laughed at the invitation and told her about all the times I had tried to serve on a mission team but the Lord hadn't let me. Her encouragement to try again had me signing up online for a week in Haiti, helping with a camp for children who live in three orphanages.

Weeks ticked closer to the departure without issues. I updated my vaccinations, bought gifts to take to the children, and packed my suitcase. The departure day arrived. I cried as I sat on the plane, readying for takeoff. Finally. Thank you, Lord.

I tell this story often, not only because of the sheer delight of going on a mission trip but also because the Lord blessed me after long-postponed obedience. Obedience to take care of me, then serve the one beside me. Being obedient to where He called me, where I was.

He had called me to write, and I didn't obey for quite a while. I allowed the emotional toxins to stop me. Getting rid of the doubt and discouragement, I had to do it scared. Not fearful, but with a bit of anxiety.

I obeyed and wrote the book He called me to write. He blessed me with serving in Haiti, a long-awaited dream. Serving children. For Him.

In Haiti, the Lord pressed on my heart about our need to submit to Him, take care of ourselves, and serve the one. My story hasn't unfolded as I thought it would, but God's rewrite has glorified Him and showed me the need for self-care and service to others.

I've been on a few more mission trips since that first one. God not only opened the door to travel, but He also opened my heart to serve simply. Serve the one.

The women said to Naomi: "Praise be to the Lord, who this day has not left you without a guardian-redeemer. May he become famous throughout Israel! He will renew your life and sustain you in your old age. For your daughter-in-law, who loves you and who is better to you than seven sons, has given him birth.

–Ruth 4:14–15

The book of Ruth takes place during the time of judges, a sad time in Israel's history when there was no king, and everyone seemed to do what they wanted. God's people fell into idolatry, and He allowed their enemies to oppress them. The exact time of the events in the book of Ruth is unknown, but the story begins during a famine.

To get relief, a man named Elimelech, from Bethlehem, took his wife, Naomi, and two sons to Moab. Eventually, the two sons married Moabite women. After Elimelech died, Naomi's sons took the role as head of the house. Then things went from bad to worse. Naomi's two sons died, leaving her a childless widow in a foreign country.

The loss of her husband and her sons spiraled into catastrophe. Naomi had no way to provide for herself or her daughters-in-law, Ruth and Orpah. Disappointment and discouragement loomed heavy. Was this the end for them all?

Then Naomi heard the famine had ended in Israel. Naomi focused on her need to return to Israel, where she knew God would provide. She felt she had nothing to offer the two younger women but more despair, so she released her daughters-in-law to return to their hometown. They were free from their obligation to her. She wanted God to deal kindly with them and grant them husbands. She felt they were covered by God's covenant because they had married Israelite men. Going back to Moab would help them revise their story.

Ruth disagreed with her mother-in-law. She was committed to staying with Naomi. Orpah cut ties and returned to her family. But Ruth wanted to serve Naomi. A Moabite woman of Gentile descent and humble circumstances, Ruth made a faith-based decision to return to Israel with Naomi. She adopted the true God of Israel as her own and told her mother-in-law, "Where you go, I will go, and where you stay, I will stay. Your people will be my people, and your God my God" (Ruth 1:16).

Ruth's commitment was so deep that she preferred to be a widow and accept the challenges that accompanied widowhood rather than abandon God and Naomi. When she denounced the idolatry of her homeland, she embraced Israel's God as her own. She made a complete break with her past. Ruth was determined, and although Naomi tried to dissuade her, they returned to Bethlehem together.

Naomi reentered Israel a broken and bitter woman. She was empty-handed and discouraged. She knew the good and bad of life filter through the hand of the Lord. In His sovereignty, He sees it all. But she didn't allow her emotional burdens to override God's power.

Unbeknownst to the women, God was about to work in a big way. Time for the barley harvest in Bethlehem began. Naomi had a sprinkle of hope amid her hopelessness.

Ruth wanted to serve Naomi, to take care of her needs. She asked to go into the fields and gather fallen grain. Moses's law required landowners to provide for the poor by leaving some grain behind at harvest time so they could collect it and have food.

Enter Boaz, a wealthy relative of Naomi's husband. He was also the son of Rahab, a prostitute who hid Israel's spies and survived Jericho's collapse because of her faith. Talk about a changed script. Another story drastically altered with the glory of God.

By chance—actually, by God's design—Ruth chose to glean in Boaz's fields. No one happens to be anywhere. God worked providentially in Ruth's life and placed her in the right place at the right time. She was there to help provide for Naomi, but God was providing more than she could have imagined. The invisible work of God took place in the field while she gathered leftovers.

Do we see God in our daily tasks? In the distraction detox, we learned how to release the tethered toxins keeping us vertically challenged. We accepted the feeling and embraced the removal process. It's time to change the replay of our history of emotional distractions and continue to move forward, rewriting our story to exalt the Lord. Like Naomi and Ruth.

Boaz learned of Ruth's history from their shared family. When Boaz found out she was the woman in the field gleaning the grain left behind, he showed her compassion and offered her a supply of grain and protection. Ruth reaped the blessings of the life she had sown. Her kindness, service to her mother-in-law, and her desire to take refuge under the Lord's provision had brought her fulfillment.

When Naomi heard about Boaz's kindness, she decided to become a matchmaker. She understood the perils of widowhood and wanted to protect Ruth, to rewrite her daughter-in-law's story. Naomi's hope for the future of what could give Ruth confidence was to create a God-providing story.

She encouraged Ruth to visit Boaz while he slept on the threshing floor to protect the grain. Naomi told her that after he ate, he would be happy and grow sleepy. Ruth should visit him then.

Boaz woke to Ruth lying at his uncovered feet. She asked him to take her under his protection since he was "a guardian-redeemer of our family." In essence, she made a marriage proposal and asked him to perform his family duty. Boaz had been impressed with her when he saw her in the field, then again with her request. He promised to take action.

Ruth remained strong in character and faithful to God. Hope rose in Naomi again. God was providing. But Boaz was not the first man in line to be the family redeemer.

As a family redeemer, the man fulfilled the law decreeing if an Israelite man were to die without having a son as an heir to carry his family name, the man's brother, or the man next in line could provide for the family by marrying the widow. The practice ensured that a man's lineage continued if he had no heirs. (Remember the Samaritan woman? That law may have resulted in her multiple marriages.)

Boaz, along with ten elders and witnesses, met with the unnamed man who had first rights to the land owned by Naomi's husband and to Ruth's hand in marriage. When the man realized he would have to marry Ruth, he declined.

Boaz was next in line, so the man gave Boaz his sandal as a symbolic custom granting him the legal right to redeem the property and Ruth. The climax of the story. The tale of disappointment ends with hope and redemption.

Boaz's selfless sacrifice to serve as the redeemer and Ruth's sacrifice for Naomi grew out of their concern for others. Blessings often flow when we lay down our priorities for the sake of God's kingdom.

Boaz and Ruth married. When Ruth gave birth to a son, the women in the village gave Naomi the blessing.

The biblical number of seven indicates perfection or completion. Seven sons would have been a supreme blessing. By God's grace, Ruth became an even better godsend.

Boaz and Ruth's marriage laid out a lineage of blessings and fulfillment. Ruth was blessed with a son, Obed, which placed her in the Messiah's family line. She became the grandmother of King David, the ancestor of Jesus.

God went to great lengths to ensure Jesus was legally qualified to be Israel's Messiah and Savior of the world. God can take messes and make miracles to advance His kingdom.

How does our story affect God's plan and purpose? Naomi's story didn't play out as planned. She became a widow and childless. She took care of herself and served her daughters-in-law as well. Ruth then stepped in, serving God, sacrificing, and providing for herself and Naomi by going to Boaz. He stepped in to redeem the family.

One serving one.

Their stories were changed for God by serving God and sacrificing for the one. When we allow God to change our story, He changes history. A changed script crafts Her-story.

We can remain strong in character and faithful to God even when society around us is uncontrollable. When we live a life free of emotional barriers, our connection to God is more profound.

We are called, as Christians, to show compassion to others. Because we have a loving heart, we want to decrease someone else's suffering.

Jesus had compassion for many. With our connection to Him and as we grow more like Him, we overflow with care. Jesus wants us to change our story. Then we can help change someone else's story. We can change the world—one person at a time.

The first is you. Self-care is not selfish. Taking care of your spiritual health is imperative. Your connection to the Lord allows His compassion to pour into you. Don't let the shame of taking care of yourself keep you imprisoned.

If you feel a little uncomfortable about self-care, I want to help you move past the awkward feeling. Going back to the tethered toxins, we learned how the emotional barriers keep us from prioritizing God's best. We cannot move forward when we allow the walls to block our spiritual health. Barriers obstruct peace and freedom.

Rewrite your history of poor choices. Take those thoughts captive, focus on Jesus, and move forward. Where is God calling you? Whom is He calling you to serve?

Earlier I talked about sandpaper people. Do you know an annoying person who drains your energy and frays your last nerve? Yes, that one. Is that who God is calling you to serve, and you refuse because it doesn't make you feel good? We have to put our comfort aside and sacrifice our energy to show the love of Christ to the one.

Are you serving in your backyard? Yes, we have needy people here in the United States. People who need Jesus. Those who need help with food insecurities. A mom with a need for an extra set of hands. How are you helping rewrite their story into a testimony of God's goodness?

Many organizations and families need volunteers. It costs no money, but it does require a sacrifice from you. Pour out your heart, time, and help. Be Naomi to Ruth. Ruth to Naomi. Boaz to the family.

You are an answer to prayer for someone. Keep an eye out for whom God is pointing you to stand in the gap. Take out your pen and begin to revise your story. Help another person's story.

My heart exponentially grew when God allowed me to visit another country and serve Him and the community. Visiting the three orphanages in Haiti was the beginning of a great partnership with an organization that provides love, education, and clean water.

These children have been put in the orphanage by parents or other family members or their relatives have died. My heart broke for what these children had lost. Some of their families were so desperately poor that their only option was to leave their children with a community that could give them what the family could not.

A year after my trip to Haiti, I took a Compassion International trip to a country we've lived in and love deeply. I knew the communities I visited with Compassion through previous experiences with other organizations. However, I hadn't seen deep needs met as I did on that trip. Compassion works through the local churches to identify children in need. Through sponsorship, they provide the sponsored child with food, medical care, education, and Christ-centered guidance.

We sponsored a girl through Compassion's sponsorship program, and I also presented the option for others to sponsor a child when I spoke at events. I knew what the organization provided, but the reality of seeing the churches, children, and the amazing staff was even more impactful.

I couldn't stop talking about the fantastic opportunities to serve those in need when I returned to the US. A year later, David and I traveled with a group of friends back to the Dominican Republic. Scripts were changed during our time there—the stories of the friends who traveled with us and those of the children, workers, and pastors of the programs we visited. God-glorifying. God's best-written plan.

Our life story may not have happened exactly how we dreamed. It may be a tale of terrible experiences or beautiful backstories or somewhere in between. We may have orchestrated the drama or taken a detour from God's plan for a while.

You can change the story with God, starting today. Continue your spiritual health plan, including serving the one. Begin with yourself, then expand to one more. And one more.

God's rewrite of our story is rewarding.

Change your story.

Change her story.

Change history to God-glorifying actions and realize God's best.

Detox Challenge

- Always begin with prayer.
- Pull out the fun, inspirational journal you use for the Detox Challenge.
- Get a sparkly pen.
- Spiritual Health Plan for today.
  - Pray.
  - Read God's Word. Pull out your Bible, Bible app, or an audio version you can listen to while on the go.
  - Hear His voice in the scripture.
  - What in your past do you need to leave behind to begin the new narrative?
  - Name one thing you need to start doing for yourself in your Spiritual Health Plan.
  - Pray about the person God wants to pair you with to help change her history to a God-glorifying story.
  - Write in your journal the person's name God is asking you to step into the gap for and with.
  - Pray about how you can serve one more person in a foreign country or area other than your own.
  - Write in your journal where God is leading you to support or serve.
  - What rewards do you see as you redirect your story to include God's guidance?
  - Write a list of things you are seeing and thank God for the blessings.

CHAPTER 12
Leave Fingerprints

The days after losing my sister and brother-in-law were extremely difficult. Watching my nephews grieve was heart-wrenching. My siblings mourned differently, but we were all heartbroken. My sons traveled to be with us, and the sadness in their eyes was painful. As a family, we embraced, yelled, cried, laughed, and stayed quiet. Sometimes all within minutes.

Watching my mother grieve was devastating. Mama battled forgetfulness along with the stages of grief—denial, anger, bargaining, depression, and acceptance. She didn't accept the truth, but at least she knew it.

Mama was adamant about writing the obituary. She wanted everyone to know Helen and Larry's legacy and to leave a written record of their existence, their contribution to society. She wanted others to understand that their lives mattered.

A few days after the disaster, my nephews chose to honor their parents with a celebration of life at the high school baseball field. Helen and Larry had been active in the booster club. Their son, my nephew, had played baseball in high school. My sister and brother-in-law helped out at every game. The ballpark was a second home.

The celebration scheduled for 3:00 p.m. started late. Cars lined the roads as friends and acquaintances tried to get into the ballpark. So many came to honor lives well lived.

The seating capacity was 1,200, and the stadium was over half full. A few people close to Helen and Larry were asked to speak. A pastor friend shared experiences of talking with them about faith. Another focused on personal interactions. One of Larry's fishing buddies told many fish tales. Bagpipes played "Amazing Grace." Larry's brother and nephew sang a hymn. I represented our family.

The night before the event, I searched for a quiet place—hard to find at Mama's house—and found a corner where no one could see me. I cried. I asked God to choose someone else. "I'm the baby of the family. Why me?" I was honored my nephews asked, but the task seemed too hard. I couldn't do it without God's help.

The few days we spent going through what survived the fire took us down a lane of memories. When a picture was funny and uplifting, we shared a funny story. Their wedding album, virtually unharmed, crushed us—the innocence of their young lives joined together as one. A picture of the trailer where they began their marriage was captioned, "Now." Under that, a picture of the barn Helen had always wanted to renovate was captioned, "Forever." Her forever home would be where she lost her life. Too much to handle sitting at the site of the ash and soot.

Those memories flooded my spirit as I sat alone, bargaining with God. Then I offered a different prayer. "Lord, let the words I speak at the celebration of life be laced with your love. Let them be your words. Jesus, guide me where you want me to go in honoring them."

Peace filled my spirit. I knew what to say. The words to honor them flowed into notes on my phone. I could do it with God's help. Only with Him could any of us go forward.

The first steps of moving forward began during the service.

When it was time to speak, I took a deep breath, stepped forward, and prayed silently for God's peace. Each of the speakers before me had told recent stories of Helen and Larry. I started from the beginning.

Helen was eight years older than I. When she got her driver's license, Mama sent me uptown with her when she ran errands. I hated those outings. Helen talked to each person she saw. A fifteen-minute errand could take two hours. Helen never saw a stranger, as they say, and she took time to love each person she saw.

For an eight-year-old who wanted to be home playing, the trips uptown were torture. My anger built because I felt we were wasting precious time I could use to run around the farm. Jealousy grew because I wanted to be as caring as she was when she took priceless time with others.

I met Larry a few years later. He was the first cousin of my oldest sister's husband. He had recently experienced a bad breakup with a longtime girlfriend. Every Friday night, my oldest sister, her daughter, and I went skating. We invited Larry to go with us, trying to shake him from his sadness.

After a few weeks of skating with Larry, I had an idea. Helen didn't have a boyfriend. Larry was single and sad. What if? We went hard on him, encouraging him to ask Helen for a date. After a few visits to Helen's retail job, he got up the nerve to ask her out.

Their relationship had been conceived in a ten-year-old mind. I thought they'd be a great couple, and I'd have them both all the time.

God knew they belonged together.

Soon after they started dating and until their passing, every time we asked Helen to do something, she had to ask Larry—not because he demanded it but out of respect for their relationship. They were always together.

At the celebration of life service, I read the vows they recited at their wedding in the Episcopal church where we grew up. "In the name of God, I take you to be mine to have and to hold from this day forward, for better, for worse, for richer, for poorer, in sickness and health, to love and to cherish, until we are parted by death. This is my solemn vow."

They broke one of these vows. They went together, never parted by death. Their marriage had meaning.

In closing, I encouraged everyone to laugh like Larry, love like Helen, and live life to the fullest. Our days are numbered.

I believe my words honored who they were and the impact they had on the lives of others. They grew their life together. The journey wasn't perfect or struggle-free, but their lives left memories and fingerprints. I was honored to share my memories at the celebration of their lives.

Our legacy is a blueprint of what God has done in and through our lives. The words spoken about my sister and brother-in-law laid out the map of the lives they touched and the work they did. Fingerprints left on the hearts of the community.

Each of us is on earth to make an imprint on life. I pray I live my life to leave a legacy, not of what I accomplish but of what Jesus has done in and through my life. We do not know when the Lord will call us home. Embrace today. Realize God's best.

As we've worked through the distraction detox, we've committed to removing the emotional barriers, restructuring our priorities, and realizing God's best. Not our best, but His. God's fingerprints are all over our lives. We only have one life for God to work in and through us. Create a blueprint from the fingerprints of His love, mercy, and grace.

I could have let the loss of my father during my adolescence, three miscarriages after the birth of two sons, a failing marriage at the ten-year mark, or the deaths of my sister and brother-in-law direct my story. But I want to use the opportunities and the tragedies God lays before me to create a legacy of His work. Choosing Jesus, His grace, and mercy has rewritten my story and history.

For if you remain silent at this time, relief and deliverance for the Jews will arise from another place, but you and your father's family will perish. And who knows but that you have come to your royal position for such a time as this?

–Esther 4:14

The book of Esther begins with Queen Vashti's refusal to obey an order from her husband, King Xerxes. She was banished, and the search for a new queen began. A decree was issued for all the beautiful young women in the empire to come to the king.

Mordecai, Esther's older cousin, was a government official. He suggested his cousin be included. After the king considered all the women, he chose Esther and crowned her queen. She gained favor in the eyes of everyone who saw her. Mordecai encouraged her to keep her race quiet.

God was at work in the choice.

During Mordecai's service at the palace, he uncovered a conspiracy and stopped an assassination plot. But his bravery was not rewarded. Haman, an ambitious and self-serving man, became second in command. Mordecai refused to bow to Haman, who thought he deserved more respect from Mordecai, a Jewish man. Haman was furious Mordecai didn't heed his commands.

Determined to destroy Mordecai and eliminate an entire Jewish race, Haman deceived the king and persuaded him to issue a decree condemning the Jews to death.

Racial hatred is always a sin. We, as Christians, must never condone it in any form. Every human on earth has worth through Jesus Christ. God created each of us in His image. His people must stand against racism when and where it occurs.

The king's decree included all the provinces in his kingdom, which included the land of Israel. If Haman's plan succeeded, all God's chosen people would be exterminated.

When Esther heard of the proclamation, she chose to risk her life to save her people. God's plans cannot be stopped. The Jewish race could not be destroyed since the Messiah had to come from the tribe of Judah. Esther and Mordecai were determined to step into the tale Haman wished to accomplish. They allowed God to write the ending, even if it was difficult.

God is not specifically mentioned in the book of Esther. However, Mordecai and Esther expected a divine deliverance. The text may not name God, but His fingerprints are all through the book. Esther and Mordecai believed in God's care, and because they acted at the right time, God used them to save His people.

Esther invited King Xerxes and Haman to a banquet where the king asked her what she really wanted. He vowed to give her anything. She invited them back to a banquet the next day.

Later that night when the king was reading over some records, he found the account of the assassination plot Mordecai had foiled and was surprised Mordecai had never been rewarded for his deed. In the morning, King Xerxes asked Haman what would be the proper way to thank a hero. Haman thought the king was talking about him, so he described a lavish reward. Shocked to learn the hero was Mordecai, Haman was humiliated.

During the second banquet, the king again asked Esther what she desired. She told him someone had plotted to destroy her and her people. She named Haman as the offender. Immediately, King Xerxes sentenced Haman to death.

Mordecai took over Haman's position, and the Jews were protected. Because of Esther's courageous act, a whole nation was saved. She saw an opportunity to act, and she seized it. Her life made a difference— ordained by God, acted on by her.

God has prepared us to leave His fingerprints along our life journey. Watch for these moments. With God in charge, we have courage. He guides us through obstacles in our lives, displaying His power as we carry out His will. With each step we take in faith, we unite our life's purposes to God's purpose. His hand in it all.

God controls the unfolding of history. He never gets frustrated by any obstacle or human action. He saves us from the evil of the world. He delivers us from sin and death. Because we trust Him, we do not fear what people may do to us. We live courageously confident in His control.

We may feel helpless when we're overwhelmed. Esther and Mordecai resisted the emotional barrier and acted with confidence.

Not only did they believe God was in control, but they also acted with self-sacrifice and courage, following God's guidance.

They laid out a blueprint to save their people. Their actions left the marks of God all over the events and demonstrated His sovereignty and love. Mordecai and Esther saw an opportunity for God's best.

We don't know the number of days we have on earth, but God has placed us where and when for Him. For now.

In baseball, young wives and moms ask for advice on marriage, parenting, and living the baseball life. Players' wives fall in the 22 to 34 age group. I've gone from their age group over thirty years ago to the grandparent stage.

One piece of advice I give is to live today as if it's your last. Last in the game. Last in life. God has positioned us in this game, city, and seat at this time to glorify Him. Embrace the opportunity.

My sister didn't know it was her last day. She'd bought gallons of butter beans the day before to freeze and to share with Mama. The beans were still in a cooler in the back of Larry's truck. We don't know how many days we have.

During struggles, hardships, and storms in our lives, difficulty reigns. But God. He wants us to allow Him to write our story during these times. He provides an opportunity for us to overcome the obstacles and find peace. We should be looking for occasions to serve Him where we are.

His fingerprints leave a trail of His mercies. Allow Him to make marks on your story. He is ready to lay down the blueprint of your life and His plan.

We've learned how to move forward when we find ourselves in the emotional storm of thoughts that don't align with God's mercies. Continue the detox. Embrace the process as much as needed. Over and over.

God has created us to impact His kingdom, not by our power but by His plan. We create a legacy—not ours but what we allow Jesus to do in and through our lives. God writes the script directing us to act on and live out.

There is a price. We must sacrifice our self-imposed narrative, self-focused desires, and a self-centered plan. Calculate the cost. When Esther was presented with the risk of her life versus the risk of an entire race of people, she chose to step into the responsibility.

Not many of us will be asked to step into a life-threatening risk, but a tough choice may feel like it. The cost of allowing God to use us where we are when He desires to do so is worth the sacrifice we make.

When faced with the decision to leave an impact for Jesus, three questions lay out our strategy.

What Does It Matter?

Asking this sets the direction of our decision. We've learned to take thoughts captive and replace them with God's Word. Connecting with scripture allows us to hear God's guidance and understand what matters. We don't always realize what is important until after the fact. But if we're honest, we have a gut feeling about what is best when making decisions that direct God's story.

Human opinion has no weight against the divine seal. What matters is the mark God places on His best. God's plan and purpose work in and through our story and leave His fingerprints—the reason He has put us on earth and what He is doing in our lives.

Getting rid of the distractions that keep us focused on the wrong things allows us to see Jesus more clearly. See His direction. Feel His presence. Satan will try to distract us with what doesn't matter. Stay connected. We are here for His glory.

Prioritizing the impact of Jesus helps us make a decision quicker. Setting our primary concern on serving the Lord first keeps our eyes focused on what is important. Making ourselves look good doesn't matter. When we work at something for others to see how well we do it, it isn't important in God's eyes.

We center our lives on Him, prioritizing Him over self. Our history should continue to show His hand, not our wishes.

We often believe the more significant the impact seen by the world, the better the outcome for Jesus. If it isn't grand, it doesn't matter. But what matters is placing God first.

What Does It Mean?

Does our strategy consider what it will mean to the Lord, to others, to us? What is the impact? Prepare to step out in faith. Many people talk about leaving a legacy so the world remembers them. Instead, we should be learning how to shape a life full of meaning so the world remembers Jesus working through us. With Jesus, our greatest days are ahead of us. Not perfect but peaceful. No longer fearful but fulfilled.

It is hard to see meaning when we're in the middle of a situation, much like when we question if something matters. But we will be rewarded in heaven when we remain steadfast in the trials. Not by our power but through His.

We mean a lot to God, and what we do for Him means His plan is in place. See the fruit in what He's asking us to do. We have His love, mercy, the fruit of the Spirit, the Holy Spirit living in and through us. We don't have to earn them.

Acting on God's call means we are a part of His plan and purpose, leaving His fingerprints. Even when it doesn't look like the story being written is a win, the process means something.

What Is My Decision?

We have a decision to make: choose Jesus or choose our thoughts and emotional barriers that stop us from embracing His best.

Determine the course of action. Even when we don't know exactly what God desires, we can take a step of faith. We move ahead boldly. We have boldness in Christ, like a lion. We proclaim the gospel and teach about Jesus with less difficulty. With courageous confidence. Eyes focused on Jesus, listening to His gentle whisper or His booming voice. If things don't work out or stop, we redirect our story with understanding and wisdom.

Decide the next step, overcome obstacles, and commit to allow

God to control the outcome. His best. In this, we see what God wants us to do next.

We have one lifetime for God to work through us. We can stay silent, or we can embrace our royal position as a child of God, the one true king, to do His work. He has prepared a place and time, an opportunity, for us to achieve His best. He uses our circumstances to leave His mark on history. We must take courage, choose to act, and execute His plan.

The strategy behind asking these three questions is to help leave His fingerprints, His legacy, on our lives. Don't miss an opportunity to serve God because of drama, wrong choices, or negative thoughts.

Our lives are stories in progress. Only God can provide the best plot line, even if it is rocky and unexpected. Today could be our last chance to make a mark, have an impact for God. Make it good.

Give Jesus the pen, the ability to guide your history. Create an existence written by God and acted on by you. What does it matter? What does it mean? What is my decision?

Move. Act. Leave His fingerprints along the way.

As you face each day, seek to know what God wants you to do, then do it, confident He will do His part. You may not know ahead of time how He will accomplish His Will, but trust God and prepare to be surprised by the ways He demonstrates His trustworthiness.

Take care of today. You were made for such a time as this.

Detox Challenge

- Spiritual Health Plan
  - Pray.
  - Read God's Word. Pull out your Bible, Bible app, or an audio version you can listen to while on the go.
  - Hear His voice in the scripture.
  - Pull out the fun, inspirational journal you use for the Detox Challenge.
  - Use a sparkly pen.
  - What in your history do you need to leave behind?
  - Name one thing you are doing for yourself.
  - Whom has God paired you with?
  - How are you serving someone in a foreign country or area other than your own?
  - Write these in your journal.
- Strategy
  - Where is God calling you to be bold?
    - What does it matter?
    - What does it mean?
    - What is my decision?
  - Decide how you will act with boldness.
  - Write these actions in your journal.
  - Take the first step in faith.

CHAPTER 13
I Dare You!

The smell of popcorn filled the terminal. My stomach rumbled, my mouth watered, but my desire to sleep once I boarded the plane stopped me from buying the buttery bucket.

I had all I needed—a mandatory travel pillow, blanket, water bottle, earphones, and a sleep mask. The last two items signaled those sitting near me that I didn't want to talk.

I love to meet new people, hear their stories, share hope and encouragement. But I know how to read the signs not to talk and hoped that vibe radiated from me.

All I wanted was six hours of sleep on the flight to the West Coast. Spending a week with our college-aged son in New York City, attending baseball games, and having late dinners had taken its toll.

The gate agent announced my boarding group. I entered the plane, glad to see not many had boarded, which provided a better opportunity to fake sleep until I slipped into a deep slumber.

As I approached my row, a man already occupied the aisle seat. He wore a Yankees ball cap and a crisp white button-up shirt. His spicy cologne tickled my nose.

I pointed to my seat. He stood and stepped out of the way so I could enter the row. I took my window seat, 11A—a better spot to lean on my travel pillow and shut the world out.

I retrieved and unfolded my travel blanket across my lap, put the water bottle in the seatback pocket, and placed my backpack under the seat in front. The man in 11C smiled but didn't speak.

Once settled in, I put an earbud in my ear. I held the second earbud in my hand when a woman two rows in front of us lost her grip as she tried to stuff her oversized carry-on in the overhead compartment. The bag fell hard on the head of the man below.

"Wow, people pack way too much in these little suitcases," the man in 11C said, staring straight ahead. He wasn't speaking directly to me, but I responded.

"That's why I don't sit in the aisle seats." My response opened the door to a question.

"Do you live in New York?"

"No, just visiting my son at NYU."

"Are you going to the West Coast for business?"

"No, my husband is working there this weekend. I'm joining him."

Really, God? I didn't want to talk to a stranger. I wanted to sleep. Then deep in my soul, I heard the Lord say, *Talk.*

I may have even sighed deeply in response, like a three-year-old who doesn't want to wash their chocolate-covered face. I took out the earbud, removed my sleep mask that rested on my forehead, and repositioned myself to face my seatmate.

We talked about NYU. He was an attorney in New York City. Our team hotel was on the same block as his office. The conversation was topical, nothing too deep. I still hoped for a bit of sleep.

The flight attendant announced the door to the plane had closed. No one had claimed the middle seat. I rolled my eyes. If someone had sat there, the row would be cramped, but the chatter would be blocked. So unlike me to resist conversation, but tired Billie knows how to keep quiet.

The man in 11C and I sat wordless for a minute, but the Lord urged me to ask why my seatmate was going to the West Coast. He took a deep breath, his eyes glassed over with tears not quite escaping—a man ready to burst forth with a story.

Sleep would not be coming.

He began with "My son became extremely ill at fourteen years old."

My heart broke, and my drowsiness became unimportant. God had placed me in an encounter that only He could have initiated.

"I'm so sorry. Tell me more."

During our conversation, he told me he'd never shared so much about his son's illness with anyone other than family. He said he felt peace and comfort talking with me. Our interaction came easily.

I shared my faith, writing, and speaking, and how David and I believe God placed us in baseball as our mission field. A typical conversation I have with strangers.

"This seat assignment was from the hand of God," he said as he leaned his head back on the seat.

"I believe Jesus does that a lot. I'm thankful He ordained us to sit together." I smiled.

I asked if he was a man of faith. He removed the baseball cap to reveal a yarmulke—a kippah or skullcap—an Orthodox Jewish man wears.

I was stunned. I had shared a lot about my Christian faith, not knowing he was Jewish. Had I offended him? When I expressed my apologies for oversharing, he wasn't upset at all—quite an unusual seatmate.

Over the next few hours, he asked me questions about my Christian faith. I asked him questions about his faith. It was the most open, respectful conversation I'd ever had with someone of a different religion.

We agreed on much and didn't disagree like I thought we would. He shared his family's history during World War II and how his faith is a family legacy. He shared stories of the pain his family endured during the Holocaust and afterward. I talked about the healings Jesus performed and continued to offer.

"Could you pray for my son to be healed?" he whispered as he leaned over the middle seat.

"I will be praying," I assured him.

"I will be also praying for the work you and your husband do as you serve the Lord in baseball and beyond."

I was convinced this man would pray for us.

"Thank you." I touched his arm as I silently prayed.

"I thank God for what you are doing in baseball and in life," he said. Heartfelt words spoken with respect and honor.

We exchanged contact information. I promised to keep praying for healing as his family walked the unknown road of medical care for his son.

My flight was nothing like I thought it would be. I didn't get sleep until the last hour of the flight. But I met a new friend who now knows more about Jesus. I learned more about the Orthodox Jewish faith. I prayed for the man, his son, and their family as I drifted off.

I almost missed a divine opportunity when I boarded that plane because my comfort and desires were more important than speaking into the life of a hurting soul.

When God spoke to me, my groaning and eye-rolling were childish reactions to a mighty God. When He directed me to speak, it was like He said, "I dare you."

Some of my most extraordinary opportunities to share the gospel, God's love, mercy, encouragement, and hope have happened in the strangest places with different people. Not the time or place I would have planned or the people I had in mind.

In fulfilling God's desires in our life, we often find ourselves among the peculiar. He challenges us to step out in faith toward the unusual, the strange, the uncomfortable.

I felt more alive in my faith after sharing with the man in 11C. I was prepared to share with him because I wasn't carrying emotional barriers caused by life's obstacles. I had been digging deep into scripture to build my confidence in knowing God's Word.

I decided this man was worth sleep loss, discomfort, or giving up my selfish intents. I spoke with boldness and courage. Peace filled me as I shared my faith journey and the Lord's goodness.

The strange meeting on an overnight flight became one of my fondest travel memories. The unusual seatmate initiated deep conversations that ended in tears and hope. God's love shines bright in unique situations.

When Joseph woke up, he did what the angel of the Lord
had commanded him and took Mary home as his wife.

–Matthew 1:24

Joseph plays such an interesting role in the story of Jesus coming
to earth. The people of Israel were waiting for the Messiah, their king.
The book of Matthew begins with a genealogy—the proof Jesus was
a descendant of David. In the line was Jacob, father of Joseph, the
husband of Mary, mother of Jesus.

In biblical times, marriages had stages. The betrothal, or formal
engagement, was a legal contract and included a ceremony with
witnesses. Then the couple returned to their parents' homes without
consummating their relationship. Joseph and Mary were under a legal
contract to marry, as binding as marriage itself.

During this time of betrothal, Mary became pregnant. Joseph was
a righteous man with strong beliefs. His respect for Mary's character
and the story she told him must have made it hard to believe she
deceived him. The child was not his, of that he was sure. However, he
didn't want to disgrace her publicly. He decided that the right thing to
do was to act in love and justice and quietly divorce Mary.

But before he could carry out his plan, God sent an angel to Joseph
in a dream. The angel confirmed Mary's story and challenged Joseph
with an unusual act of obedience. Peculiar circumstance. Unusual
incident. Unexpected people.

Angels are divine messengers. One of their duties is delivering God's
message to humans. The angel told Joseph to take Mary as his wife. The
baby, a son, had been conceived by the Holy Spirit—the biggest miracle
in human history. God became man. Immanuel, God with us.

Joseph was to give the boy the name Jesus, which means "the Lord saves." Jesus came to earth to save us because we cannot save ourselves from our sins and their consequences. Jesus came to be our Savior, and He is present today in the life of every believer.

God planned for Joseph to be Jesus's earthly father. All these events were not unexpected happenings. They were fulfillments of the Old Testament prophecy.

When Joseph woke from the dream, his plans changed.

Mary had not been unfaithful, and this birth was a miracle. Joseph did what he was supposed to do. A great calling.

I've always felt for Joseph. He finds himself in an unexpected circumstance. Mary's story is unusual. God asks him to do something extraordinary. He was not in the perfect place at the ideal time to make an impact the way he probably thought he was going to make.

But he was a faithful man who listened to God. He took a risk and obeyed, even when he didn't understand all that would happen.

In scripture, we see many people who found themselves in situations they didn't think were the right place or the exact time. They didn't think they were suitable people for God to use. And every time God used them to do more extraordinary things than they could imagine.

Job struggled more than most humans, but he didn't deny God. He persevered and showed others God's greatness. His three friends weren't people he wanted to hear, but he listened. God used Job to encourage many.

David was the youngest of Jesse's sons, not the one his father thought was exceptional. He defeated a giant with a slingshot, was chosen by God, and was anointed as king. For years David ran from King Saul, but David continued to listen to the Lord. He did the next thing God asked him to do. He wasn't perfect—he committed adultery and killed men. But David is known as Israel's greatest king and a man after God's heart. He went on to write about half of the book of Psalms.

In unusual places, imperfect humans laid the foundation for Jesus Christ—the only sinless human, who God used to save all of humanity.

Esther, a Jewish woman, was placed in a palace as queen. She helped God save the Jewish race. Again, circumstances were unexpected. The outcome was not all her responsibility, but she was invited to be a part of God's perfect plan.

God tested Abraham. He was told to take his son Isaac to Mount Moriah to offer him as a sacrifice. This is one of the craziest stories in the Bible. As a parent, I wonder who on earth would follow this command.

Abraham did. He saddled his donkey, cut the wood, and took his son Isaac. When Isaac asked what they were doing, Abraham told him they were offering a sacrifice.

Isaac questioned why they had no lamb. Abraham said God would provide. Here was Abraham walking in obedience to God and Isaac trusting his father. Just as the sacrifice of Isaac was about to be fulfilled, God intervened. Because Abraham had not withheld his son and had offered him to the Lord, God promised to bless Abraham. And He did. Abraham became the father of the promised nation, Israel.

Miriam assumed the responsibility of keeping an eye on her baby brother, Moses. He was sent down the river in a basket. When Pharaoh's daughter found him, Miriam approached her and offered a Hebrew nursemaid—her mother, Jochebed. Much later, Miriam stood by Moses's side, leading people in worship. She was not perfect, but after God corrected her, she continued to serve her people.

Mary, the mother of Jesus and wife of Joseph, was a teenager when God chose her to carry the baby that would save the world. She was committed to being the Lord's servant. She had to tell her betrothed, Joseph, she was pregnant. She watched her son be celebrated by the three wise men; years later, she watched as he was mocked by soldiers and crucified on a cross. The risks Mary took allowed her to experience the miraculous and traumatic with a heart that trusted God.

Eve impacted the world as the first mother. Sarah was the mother of a nation of people. Rebekah, another imperfect mother, influenced the future. Rachel's and Leah's children became the heads of the twelve tribes of Israel. Leah was the mother of Judah, who led the tribe that produced the genealogical line of Jesus.

Miriam helped her mother, Jochebed. Jochebed helped Pharaoh's daughter. Deborah, the only female judge of Israel, inspired people with her faith and wisdom.

Ruth sacrificed her homeland for Naomi, and Naomi helped Ruth find a husband. Rahab harbored the Hebrew spies for her family's safety, which played a crucial role in God's plan of salvation. Esther's courage saved the Jewish people from destruction. Mary reached out to Elizabeth. Elizabeth rejoiced with Mary.

In many of these peculiar situations, God used unlikely people in uncertain times. They took risks, which ultimately led to the birth of Jesus, our Savior. Jesus died for sinners, for us—the most peculiar part of God's plan. In Jesus's sacrifice, we have been given a gift we do not deserve—grace, forgiveness, salvation. Because of the gospel, we can step out in faith with courageous confidence to begin the story God has for us.

All of these faith Hall-of-Famers were courageous. They took chances by going into odd experiences with unusual people to serve the Lord, honoring and worshipping God along the way. Yes, there were hiccups and obstacles, but they persevered without a clear path to the outcomes.

If you haven't read these stories in the Bible, I encourage you to take a look. These stories are fantastic and offer encouragement. We are not the first generation to go through tough experiences. The lives of these people illustrate how to move forward when we find ourselves in an odd situation.

What if God calls us to fulfill His desire in a strange place or with an unusual command? In fulfilling God's purpose for our life, we may find ourselves among the peculiar, which includes me. We do not have to be perfect or have it all together to serve the Lord where we are when He asks.

We fulfill His calling by loving the outsiders who are looking in, those who may not be or look like us. We are all children of God, in need of a Savior. No matter how imperfect we are, we serve a perfect God. We can show His love for others.

Take a risk. The gospel enables us to love the unusual and step into realms we never thought we could. We feel alive when we fulfill God's call. We step out in boldness to be prepared, to decide, and to begin.

Prepare. Be willing to step into a new situation to glorify God at any time. To equip yourself, read scripture and communicate with the Lord through prayer. Live in the confidence that God is ready to use you if you allow Him. Watch for opportunities. Be ready. Prepare to make a move.

Decide. When the opportunity arises to share your faith or encourage someone, say yes. Before you say yes, be aware of what to say no to.

What are we saying no to? No to external distractions. No to internal distractions. No to negativity. No to things that stop us. Create a response of no without guilt or fear.

What are we saying yes to? Yes to the Lord. Yes to glorify Him. Yes to encourage someone. Yes to everything the Lord challenges us with so we become more Christlike. Decide to say yes to the awkward, the atypical person, or the untimely event.

Begin. I dare you! I dare you to be an instrument of peace. A sower of love. A forgiver. An includer. A light of faith, hope, love, and joy. A life-giver with words. An encourager. A vessel of the gospel. We feel alive when we fulfill God's desires and intentional inspiration.

"Mary responded, 'I am the Lord's servant. May everything you have said about me come true.' And then the angel left her" (Luke 1:38).

Believe He is prepared to equip you for this time and place. Know that He has a plan to prosper and not to harm. Trust He has the best in store for His kingdom. Take a chance.

He needs us to be His vessels to implement His plan. If we don't allow God to use us, that won't stop Him. He will find a way. But do we want to be a speed bump in His plan or a promoter? Be an encourager, enforcer, and engager of the gospel.

No more questioning if you want or if you can. Be courageously confident in where God is directing you. Take a risk. Obey Him in taking the first step. If that doesn't work out, take another step in a different direction.

We have to do it tired and scared. We move forward without a definite destination. We use our lack by tapping into His abundance. It is not about us. The gospel present in our lives is all about Him.

The woman at the well showed up to see Jesus, who waited for this divine appointment. He used the time to encourage a woman who felt inadequate.

Joseph honored God by taking Mary, a pregnant teen, as his wife. He was a carpenter, not a man of renown. His feelings did not guide him; the Lord led him. Joseph was obedient, which led to more guidance from the Lord, who guided him, Mary, and baby Jesus from place to place to keep them safe.

Take advantage of every opportunity. Even when you're weary, love well. Even while you suffer, encourage. Your agenda may not line up with Jesus's. Accomplish His plan anyway. Stay steadfast. Stay faithful. God is with you!

A few months after my most memorable conversation on a plane, I received an email. I didn't recognize the name, but after reading the first few lines, I realized it was the man in 11C. After a conversation with his wife about our talk, they prayed for us.

Tears dripped as I read the words he wrote: "My wife and I wanted to honor the work you and your husband are doing for your faith. We have planted a tree in Israel honoring you both." I opened the attachment. The certificate stated a tree had been planted in honor of David and Billie Jauss.

I cried, praised the Lord, and prayed for the family. What an incredibly tender show of love for us by a man I didn't want to talk to because I was tired. But I felt an urge from the Lord, took a risk, and thought I had made a complete fool of myself. Yet God connected two people of faith in a way I don't understand, and may not this side of heaven. But God used this peculiar encounter to impact both our lives. The uncomfortable situation was a worthwhile experience.

I dare you!

Take a risk.

Step into an awkward encounter and believe God will bless it.

Detox Challenge

- Begin with prayer.
- When has God asked you to take a risk?
- How did you react? What did you do?
- No excuses. No judgment.
- Take a risk for Him.
- Make a list of peculiar circumstances, unusual incidents, or unexpected encounters when you had opportunities to share the love of Jesus.
- List three scriptures to meditate on to help you leave fear, condemnation, and judgment behind as you step out in faith.
- Purposefully look for opportunities to love someone who isn't like you.
- Take a risk. Follow God's leading.

CHAPTER 14
Significant Start

The distraction detox has encouraged us to release our emotional toxins, restructure our priorities and realize God's best. The detox process has not been easy. We've put in the hard work and implemented the changes. Facing new tasks of change and executing the plan, no matter how small it may seem, helps us implement the strategies. Be the change.

Over the years, I've watched many kids, including my three sons, try to reach their lofty goal of playing on a major league baseball field. The route started with a small soft white ball and an unsteady toddler. Each son's first throw, while seated on his bum, usually resulted in the ball falling behind him. Our sons progressed and toppled over, one toddler at a time.

When they finally could stand and throw, the ball went in hundreds of directions, which led to hours of running, retrieving the errant pitches. Many times, as I helped in the progression, they made contact with my face as they ran up and threw the ball quickly.

When the boys were older, the big orange plastic fat bat made its debut. When that thing came in contact with my knees, I gave my boys a kazoo. Kazoos don't bruise your knees. They weren't excited about the small plastic toy that made noise but returned to the bats quickly.

The boys were obsessed with bats and balls or any object that could become a projectile by being thrown or hit. All three boys swung the bat with great force; they fell, got up, and ran in the wrong direction.

T-ball was their first team experience. More kids picked the clovers in the grass than paid attention to the game. My boys were the fanatics who wanted to take every at-bat and run after every ball.

When a ball was hit off the tee, the screams of parents caught the players' attention. Everyone on the team ran for the ball. A dogpile of little bodies fell on it.

The runner advanced to first. Rounding second in a large arch, she barely touched the base. Finally, she stopped at third, only to be waved home because one of the infielders was under the mound of bodies, crying.

The coaches ran to help the crying child on the bottom of the pile—crying only because his pants had a grass stain. The runner crossed home, threw her helmet aside, adjusted her hair bow and high-fived both teams' players, then ran to the wrong dugout and grabbed a juice box.

The next level for my boys was Little League, followed by Babe Ruth Baseball and high school ball. A few friends were drafted out of high school to play minor league baseball with a major league organization, while others played college baseball. Some were drafted out of college; others got paying jobs in the "real" world.

The small percentage of toddlers who become young men that get a chance to play professional baseball is tiny. But the number is finite. Statistics show that around seven percent of high school players play college ball. Only about ten percent of college players get a chance to play professionally. Professional players who make the big league teams are around seventeen percent. High school players who make the major league teams are around one-half of a percent.[7]

Our boys worked hard at baseball. They took it seriously. Two of the three played college baseball. Only one got drafted to play professionally, but he did not make it to the major leagues.

Even though their love for baseball didn't make them major league players, it did prepare them for their forever jobs. The perfect

[7] "Baseball Probability," NCAA, April 20, 2020, http://www.ncaa.org/about/resources/research/baseball-probability-competing-beyond-high-school.

place God had planned all along. Their efforts weren't wasted. God's plan was fulfilled. Two of our sons work for professional baseball organizations. The oldest is an amateur scout, the middle son a mental conditioning coach, and our youngest a college coach.

Their journey started with that tiny white squishy ball. One throw, one hit, one base at a time. Their ultimate dream wasn't achieved, but God used all their experience for good.

As a player, coach, or significant other in professional baseball, the ultimate goal is to make it to the big leagues. That is when you have arrived. However, what we know is the journey didn't begin the first day the player or coach steps onto the major league field.

Don't get me wrong. It is exciting to make it, but if that is the ultimate definition of success, we will see anything else as failure.

Nothing fails when God is in control.

David's job changed from major league coach to an off-field position a few times over the years. People reached out to express their sympathy. Fans even sent cards in the mail. The fans and friends grieved the loss of the big-league position, not just the job.

David and I know God placed us in baseball for a purpose. Every job at every level, even if seen as insignificant by others, has been given to us by God. He has placed us where He desires us to be. In each placement, He needed us to serve Him. He's a big God with grand plans.

The rookie ball position in the Gulf Coast League, minor-league coordinator, advance scout, and front-office jobs were not demotions or insignificant. No matter the role, God was positioning us. They were all beginnings to a more significant impact for the kingdom. Some took us to a quiet place to transform our lives; others helped us grow. Many assignments humbled us, taught us the value of the significance of small beginnings. We learned to expect the "immeasurably more" God desires, even in the smallest matters.

Many times, I had to discern significant versus insignificant. What I experienced compared with what others thought about my experience made me feel small. I allowed them to describe what was important, not what I knew God identified as important.

Many view a coach's wife as insignificant compared to a player's wife. Others see coaches as lacking intelligence in comparison with front-office employees. No matter what position David or I had in baseball, I felt like it was never good enough.

The views of others were assumptions and opinions of a hierarchy of importance. Overcoming other opinions is difficult. Believing we are where we need to be is a struggle.

Any new position, career change, or different city creates stress. The hardest part of any endeavor is the beginning. Are we prepared enough, smart enough, adequately equipped? The *enoughs* plague us before we start. What is God calling us to do next? The one next thing?

I've felt small. I've allowed others to make me feel like I was invisible. My heart has always urged me to care and to make a difference in the world, in God's kingdom. When I felt small, I thought my actions were insignificant—the money in the bank account minimal, my energy depleted, and my influence nonexistent. I thought my start had to be enormous to make an impact.

I would have a spark of inspiration, get all excited, and tell someone, but he or she wouldn't be as convinced. I was an ordinary person, nothing special. Or people would say the only reason it would work was because of David's job, not my effort.

The first year David made the big leagues was the most taxing financial time of our lives. We had waited ten years for the opportunity. What was it all for? The waiting. The lack of money. The terrible living situation. I was so disappointed.

I believed the influence we would have in the big leagues would be grand and impressive, but we were low on the food chain. I didn't realize we were dropping tiny seeds in the planting phase; it was not harvest time. All the years in the minor leagues with small groups prepared us to focus on what was important.

I had to begin with one small step, one decision, and one action, believing in the big God I served. Not serving myself or others first, but God. Take care of my spiritual health, understand that God was at work in it all. Then others.

Meet the challenges head-on, not fretting about how everything will work out or what obstacles might arise. Keep going. God has it all mapped out. We don't have to rely on our strength but His.

I stutter-stepped, stopped, or stumbled in the next step. Obstacles presented themselves. Kids, family, food, or chaos invaded my space. Emotional barriers lined up like participants at a barre class. Unexpected feelings were exposed.

All those emotions and experiences are normal, but I couldn't let them stop me. The obstacles became an ignition to start something beautiful. My greatest fear is not that I will fail but that I will succeed in things that don't matter. I fear my life will not matter, will lack meaning. Seeing each little place Jesus works in and through my life gives me peace and fulfillment.

"Do not despise these small beginnings, for the Lord rejoices to see the work begin."

–Zechariah 4:10

After the Hebrew people had spent seventy years in Babylonian captivity, some fifty thousand of them journeyed back to Israel, their homeland. The leader was Zerubbabel, a prince of Judah.

Another key player was Zechariah, a prophet whose task was to invigorate the spiritual lives of God's people. He received eight symbolic visions from God. In Zechariah 4, his fifth vision shows Zerubbabel that God gives divine enablement for the work He ordains.

Zerubbabel had the task of rebuilding the temple; its completion had been delayed for sixteen years. Some of the group complained the job was too difficult. Others saw the project as insignificant compared to Solomon's glorious temple.

When the older Jews realized the new temple would not match the previous temple's size and grandeur, they were disappointed. But bigger and more beautiful is not always better.

Zechariah rebuked the people for despising the small beginning, reminding them that God's Spirit accomplishes great things. He encouraged Zerubbabel not to fear the size or difficulty of the task. God's supply of power is sufficient for any and every situation.

God frequently chooses to accomplish great things through small beginnings. What we do for the Lord may seem small and insignificant at the time, but God celebrates what is right. Is there any such thing as a small deed in the hands of God?

A tiny seed scattered on the good soil produces a harvest beyond our wildest dreams.

One raindrop after another falls, providing water to keep fields irrigated and animals and humans alive.

Tiny grains of sand create beautiful beaches.

One unique snowflake falls, accumulating into feet.

A brief encounter with an encouraging person can change the trajectory of someone's life.

A smile changes the outlook of the day.

One kind word brings peace.

Jesus works in the small. A boy's lunch fed thousands. Through David's faith, a small stone brought down a big giant. The bleeding woman in the crowd had just a little faith, enough to touch Jesus's garment and be healed.

When you feel small, start there—a new beginning. See Christ. Believe in the fantastic work He desires to do in and through your life. He has your best in mind. He loves you.

God provides us with the power through His Holy Spirit to make us courageously confident. When we rely on God rather than our strength, ability, or intelligence, His magnificent work is accomplished through the Holy Spirit. God's love transforms the hardest of hearts.

Many people during Zerubbabel's time considered rebuilding the temple unimportant. With God, self-limiting thoughts and words are replaced with rejoicing. Train your mind to see the opportunity in everything, no matter the size.

God is omniscient. He knows what He's doing. His eyes wander the earth looking for the righteous people who have a relationship with Him and are committed to glorify Him in all they do. God's call on our life and the fulfillment of that call is a celebration. The Lord rejoices when we take that one small step toward rebuilding, realigning, and reconnecting.

The Lord doesn't need us to do great things. He needs us to do the one thing He is asking us to do next. God will make that one obedience as significant or as impactful as it needs to be. He is looking for ready souls. Start moving. Take that one step. Make a decision and put it into action.

The Lord sees us. He approves of the confidence we have in what He is calling us to accomplish. God will call us to do what we cannot do and will provide everything we need to do it. A meaningful life doesn't happen when we have arrived at the pinnacle point of what we believe is essential. A life of meaning starts right where we are.

Do not despise the small beginning by allowing your feelings to create a wall. Jump the hurdle and begin the work. The Lord rejoices. Overcome obstacles one at a time. Focus on the little things you can do. Those are training grounds, giving perspective, qualifying you as God's vessel, and setting your course to glorify Him. Little things can make a significant impact on the big picture.

Change the way you think, act, and move. Walk away from what you don't need to carry. It is not too late, nor too early. Start now. Don't resist the small beginnings but persist in the next thing God is calling you to. Don't give up. Persevere when you feel stuck. Hope even though there is hopelessness. Believe even when there is doubt. Find courage during discouragement.

You may not think the last chapters of a book should be about starting, but that is where we should be—starting with the small. Small beginnings. Beginning where God has us, where we live, work, and play.

Removing the emotional barriers allows us to realign our priorities. We become confident in God's call no matter the magnitude of the impact. Throw the small white squishy ball even if you don't know where it's going or fall on your bum or run in the wrong direction.

Do not resist the small beginning but persist in the next thing God is calling you to do. Decrease the distractions, refocus your priorities, and embrace the significance of the small but impactful steps that happen one at a time.

Start small and let God do it all.

We may think the world's problems, or even our problems are much too big to solve. The Lord encourages us to begin. He rejoices as we commit to the first step. Great results come from the Spirit of the Lord. The tiny moments and choices we make determine the outcomes. Be faithful in the small opportunities.

You don't have to make it to the big leagues to make an impact. Mother Teresa was a woman who knew God and how He could impact the world with her meager offerings. One person. The small beginnings of one tiny woman, not quite five feet tall, made lasting impacts all over the globe.

The mustard seed is one of the smallest seeds planted in the Middle East. In the right conditions, it can grow into a tree that gives birds a safe haven, life to other organisms. Wow, what growth. In the right conditions.

Create the right conditions. Commit to following a big God who is dropping seeds, building a foundation. Choose one person to include, inspire, and encourage—just one. We cannot change the world by reaching the thousands before we affect the life of one.

If God wants you to impact the tens of thousands, He will provide what you need as you go. But don't start there. Start with the one. The one God has given you.

If each person who reads this book inspires at least one person, many people will be reached. The number compounds over time. See what is possible by the transformation of your life and the one person you influence. One is a catalyst for what is to come.

Next, we connect where we live, work, and play. Relationship building encourages trust. Trust builds community. Community builds the kingdom of God. Investing in relationships in our neighborhood creates a group of people we can trust. They can rely on us when needs arise. We can share Jesus by loving them.

Work can be a difficult place to share our faith in an open way. If we connect to our coworkers with the outpouring of Jesus's love, they will notice. When my kids were young, my coworkers were mothers at the playground or school. Love them like Jesus. People are everywhere.

Look for the one God desires you to build a relationship with.

Last, continue on the course the Lord lays out, one step, action, or decision at a time. Jesus lights our path as we walk in faith. Sometimes the dimly lit walkway becomes confusing. Remember He is with you. Step out, take action, make a decision. Hear the Lord rejoice.

Action is a choice. Choose to begin. Zerubbabel laid the foundation of the temple. Not by his power but by the Spirit of the Lord. The Lord told Zechariah the temple would be completed. When the final stone was laid, many people rejoiced and praised the Lord. They all saw the power of the small beginnings.

What small beginnings is the Lord calling us to initiate?

A word can make an enormous impact on the life of another. *Love* is a short word—just four letters—but when shared can create a confident, joyful, and peaceful person. *Joy*, only three letters, can turn a life around. A short phrase, "You look great," can build up someone who feels broken.

Be kind with your words—one small choice.

There is power in even a little bit of time. Instead of wasting minutes, create moments. Investing our time for the love of others makes a tremendous impact on relationships and kingdom-building.

A tiny amount of humility is a step toward personal transformation. When we view ourselves with an attitude of humbleness, God can do mighty work through our lives. We are small in comparison to Him. Be humble and modest.

Faith in what God can and will do can move mountains. Investing in a childlike faith allows an openness to God and leads to His forgiveness of our mountain of sins, which He then casts into the ocean.

Perpetuate a significant start. Take the first step.

What if we choose not to take that step, make that decision, take action? Then we will never stumble across the path God is laying out in front of us. Taking small actions when we feel small or insignificant keeps our focus vertical. On God.

Begin with a great belief in the One who created you. Lasting change begins with one small step.

Do not undervalue who He created you to be. Your life is not insignificant to Him. View yourself through His lens. See the greatness of who God is and what He wants to do in and through you. He is calling you to serve Him.

Be the change you wish to see in the world. Choose one charity, organization, or group you admire and volunteer. Just start. Find a food bank, after-school or tutoring program, homeless shelter, soup kitchen, or library. Get involved with Compassion International or a mental health clinic. Volunteer for environmental cleanup or garbage pickup on a highway.

Your investment doesn't have to be financial. You have resources other than money. Make the time. Be the light in their darkness. Hold their hands in yours. Give them a foot up. Share your heart.

We all rely on our favorite map app to steer us when driving to a new destination. Miles upon miles of trusting technology to get us where we are going. Near the end of travel, the voice announces, "In one hundred feet, you will arrive at your destination." Then you hear the proclamation, "You have arrived."

We have arrived! We are right where God wants us to begin, where we're supposed to be. That new challenge is the small beginning. God is big enough to accomplish what He wants.

Each start is a significant start. Jesus is not deterred by who we think we are or are not. He doesn't keep a record of wrongs from our past. He doesn't see our differences. He focuses on the equal value of each person made in His image.

We see our lack of ability. God sees His power and strength.

You are qualified for a significant start. You don't have to have it all together to start with one small step, decision, or action.

Detox Challenge

- Begin with prayer. Pray that you will see the one next thing God desires.
- Commit to following a big God.
  - Drop seeds.
  - Build foundations.
  - Start with the one.
- Connect where you live, work, and play.
  - Build relationships.
  - Pour out God's Word.
- Continue on the course, the plan.
  - Step out.
  - Take action.
  - Redirect if needed.
- By His power, not yours.
  - Be humble.
  - Be modest.
- Make a significant start where you are.
- Be the change.

CHAPTER 15
In-Play

The most profound prayer in my life was to support David. I struggled with it because I was grieving the loss of my career. I chose to walk away from nursing because David's work schedule kept him away from home for weeks on end. I worked nights and had a babysitter who, at that point, was raising my children.

I chose to walk away from nursing because I wanted to be there for my children. David's career dreams were more extensive than mine. I tried to help him achieve those dreams as best I could. Yet, there I sat, sulking over my purpose and worth.

After putting the boys to bed one night, I felt such despair, I began to cry. Anger boiled inside of me. I made a list of all the reasons David's ability to work, when I couldn't, wasn't fair. I put together a case that could stand up against any argument he might raise.

I dared to pray to the Lord, entreating Him to be my advocate. "Make my way right. Back me up in this argument."

He gently whispered in my ear, *Is your way right?*

Of course, I was right. It wasn't fair.

Can I not use you wherever you are?

Why does God have to disagree with me? I am a work in progress, I know, but really?

Whatever you do, work for me.

Yep, that's what I'm talking about. Didn't He hear me? I want to work.

Work for me with all your heart.

I knew the scripture that was wriggling in my spirit. I grabbed my Bible, wiped my tears, and began to read it. I didn't hear the phone ringing. Our oldest answered it in the kitchen, while he grabbed a midnight snack. He walked into the room with a sandwich in one hand, jelly dripping from his chin, and extended the phone to me. "Dad."

I kissed his forehead, wiped his chin, and told him goodnight.

My conversation with David was much different than I had planned. The new desire to figure out the work the Lord had for me in my unique circumstances lit a fire to understand God's plan and purpose.

A few weeks later, David was home for several days. He took out his Bible and opened it to Colossians. He read the verse the Lord had spoken to me.

"I've decided to change my attitude toward my work," he said, then told me how his career had been about others liking him, patting him on the back, and being successful as he climbed the ranks. A new purpose filled him as he read Colossians 3. He wanted to serve the Lord in all that he did, all of his work.

I knew the Lord was taking both of us to a new level—determination to glorify Jesus wherever He placed us in whatever He called us to do.

Every day when David left for work I reminded him to have fun. He played a game for a living. Well, actually, he didn't even play. He watched a game as a job. But I wanted to make sure he kept his heart in the proper perspective. If we are working for the Lord, we will have fun.

At the end of 2019, David lost one job, then found another off the field as a scout. We didn't know if he'd be back on the field in uniform. Not a fun time for him—questioning his future in baseball. I was lost too.

My work had turned into loving on baseball wives in the stands. What would I do if I wasn't in the stands? David and I kept reminding each other that if God brought us to this place, we were to work at it for Him.

The pandemic of 2020 shut down the world but didn't slow down the thoughts spinning in my head. When the world went into lockdown, I was in Arizona speaking at an event for baseball wives and girlfriends, serving the community I loved so dearly.

The event was scheduled for Friday, the day after major league baseball canceled all spring training games. No one knew if or when anything, including baseball, would be up and running again. The baseball women gathered with much trepidation. All of us needed to focus on Jesus, not our circumstances.

The event gave us time to think about who was in control. Shortly after our time together, I think, at times, I forgot to focus on Jesus, but it was such an encouragement to be reminded of our gathering as one day led to another with no time together.

Over the next few months, I revisited the reminder of God's sovereignty many times. A tornado of chaos churned as life had come to a stop: no work, social interactions, or travel.

During the stay-at-home order, time was abundant. David and I had time to play games with each other and with our kids online. We put puzzles together, spent time with one another, and watched more movies than we had in the previous thirty years. I had so much time on my hands that the toxins I had previously removed reared their ugly heads again.

Thankfully, David and I began a daily reading of devotions. We had tried over the years to be consistent, but life always got in the way. We read a day or two in a row, then missed a week or so. While we drank our morning coffee during the stay-at-home days, we read, discussed, and shared our hearts.

If 2020 taught me anything, it was that I needed to find peace and joy each day no matter what is going on—another repeated lesson but a highly beneficial one. Peace filled my spirit during lockdown. Whatever God wanted to do, He could. I surrendered to Jesus completely. David and I served the Lord in working on our marriage, friendship, and relationship with all our hearts.

At the end of 2020, David received an unexpected call. He had an opportunity to interview for a new job on the field, to glorify God in a new place with a refreshed perspective. We are called to fulfill God's will in every opportunity He gives, no matter if that is at home or in a ballpark.

I saw the smile in my husband's eyes as he peered over the dugout in spring training. He was double-masked, but his eyes twinkled with excitement. The skip in his step coming out of the dugout made me giggle. He was having fun.

The smell of dirt and fresh-cut grass, the snap of a ball hitting a glove, the crack of a ball off the bat confirmed baseball was back. David was with a team in a dugout. The joy bubbled over in me, along with a few tears of pride.

Change and challenges aren't easy, but growth in our faith, fun, and fulfillment requires sacrifice. Only at my most profound surrender, when I humbled myself to the power of Jesus, did I see how He fulfilled my calling, my work.

When I didn't think I had an impact on the kingdom, life didn't matter. I had no purpose, yet God had a plan. I needed to plod through those discouraging times one step, decision, and action at a time. I had to leave the toxins behind because the Enemy wanted to stop me before I made an impact.

Fulfillment is achieving something desired, promised, or predicted—satisfaction or happiness resulting from fully developing our abilities or character. Our earthly profession, career, or occupation will never fulfill us. What others find essential will not give us peace.

Only through the goodness of God and His mercy can we reach fulfillment, joy, and contentment—not working for our glory but receiving God's goodness.

When David and I committed to seeing baseball as our work, His calling for us, we had to put aside our feelings. We work in baseball to please God, not others, fulfilling His purpose, not our own, wherever He places us.

God fulfilled His plan in my life when I wasn't paying attention to His calling and His purpose. The compassion I showed the woman who called and asked if she could talk to me about my faith. That one man on a plane whose faith encouraged me to be patient. At a Bible study with the women to whom God wanted to speak about gratitude.

Jesus used me in the life of my three boys. He trusted me to develop and launch their lives, teaching them compassion, kindness, and forgiveness. I wrote my first book when I didn't think I could, the second when I knew only He could—building humility. The worker at the stadium needed a listening ear. A fellow baseball wife doubted God's goodness, and I let her know she wasn't alone.

Learning someone's story. Living life with others. Doing the one thing and helping others. Listening. Hugging. Praying. Loving like Christ.

"Whatever you do, work at it with all your heart, as working for the Lord, not for human masters.
—Colossians 3:23

Paul wrote Colossians while he was imprisoned in Rome. He had never visited Colossae. Other converts from Paul's missionary travels founded the church. Some believers attempted to combine elements of paganism and secular philosophy with Christian doctrine. Paul confronts those false teachings and affirms the sufficiency of Christ.

He instructs us to live as those made alive in Christ. He encourages us to set our minds on things above, not others' opinions. Once we believe in Christ, our lives are hidden with Christ in God. We are to put to death our earthly nature of sin, placing our hearts in His hands.

Paul offers us a strategy to help us live for God one day at a time. We are told to clothe ourselves with compassion, kindness, humility, gentleness, and patience. These virtues are much needed today and always. We use the gifts God has already given us; we don't have to gather up the courage because the resources are already there.

Because of God's great love, we are not consumed by challenges. Jesus is the source of compassion. His compassions never fail. We are to show compassion and mercy to one another.

Kindness is not only listed in Colossians 3, it is also as a fruit of the Spirit. God gives us access to an unlimited supply of kindheartedness. Tapping into His kindness and presenting it to the world is our decision. Choose to be kind.

In our surrender to the Lord, we become humble. Humility comes before honor and with wisdom. We show wisdom and understanding by living a good life and doing good. When clothed with humility, we are not proud or arrogant. God lifts the humble in spirit.

To live a life worthy of our call, we are to be gentle. Gentleness is another fruit of the Spirit. Our gentleness should be evident to all. It prepares us to answer those who ask about the foundation of our joy.

We are to be patient, answering in love and bearing with one another in careful instruction. God encourages us to love as Christ loves us. Do not give up waiting on the Lord to fulfill His plan.

Clothed in all these layers, we embrace forgiveness. We forgive ourselves and others, of the past and present, as Christ has forgiven us. Through the blood of Jesus, we are cleansed of all sins, set free, and justified. We are not called to judge others but to love them with the affection Jesus does.

If we let love guide our lives, the love of Christ we experience pours out on others. This type of love is not a feeling but a decision to love the Lord and meet others' needs. It leads to the peace of Christ ruling in our hearts.

We can be thankful for all things, good and bad, because God uses them all for His glory. Gratitude opens our heart to God's peace and enables us to love. If we keep God's Word in our heart at all times, we will represent Jesus well.

Disconnected people constantly calculate what's wrong with

their lives. Connected hearts represent Christ, wherever they go and whatever they do. There is contentment.

Paul goes on to give instructions for the Christian household. He talks about the mutual responsibility to submit, love, obey, and encourage, to work hard and be fair.

I don't want to skip over the instruction to slaves. Historically slaves, or servants, were part of the household. Paul instructed the servants to do what they were told, not to work at things halfway but to put their whole effort into the tasks. He told them to work as if working for the Lord, not their earthly boss. Work from their heart, confident in serving the ultimate Master, Christ.

Paul also instructed the heads of the household to treat their servants graciously. He reminded them they serve a greater master, God in heaven. Unfortunately, we know from history that people did not follow these instructions. I continue to pray for healing.

In Colossians we are told that whatever we do, we should work at it as for the Lord. Our salvation is a gift from the Lord. We don't have to work for that. However, our actions lead to being more Christlike as we clothe ourselves with compassion, kindness, humility, gentleness, and patience.

We begin the work by putting into action the next thing God is calling us to do. Our motivation must be spiritual, producing excellence and being Christlike. God's power in action within us. Not starting over but starting where we are.

Practice makes permanent.

The intent of our actions defines the amount of the glory given to God. If we take on a task to build up our résumé or fame without making Him the focus of the work, we are not glorifying Him. An intentional walk of spiritual growth replaces our misdirected ambition with God's calling. Growing with purpose.

God began a good work in us and will bring it to completion. He can accomplish all that He desires in us and through us if we allow His Holy Spirit to work.

Christians belong to Christ and are called to be part of His redemptive work, reconciling the world to Christ and called according to His purpose—a calling much more profound than a workplace calling. Our purpose is to share the gospel through our actions, having fun as we work at it with all our hearts.

Defining our gifts and talents helps us to focus on where God uses us. What passions has He placed in our heart? Where is He already using us that we may not find essential, but He does? How can we use our talents with more commitment and confidence?

Take a risk. Look at things in a different way by using God's lenses.

Center your effort on service to others, sharing His love, grace, and mercy. Be purposeful about emulating Him with mission-driven service. As you serve the mission God has given you, leave His fingerprints as the legacy of a believer.

Even after we've made the commitment to serve God, we often question what our calling or purpose is. How do we know when we are in the sweet spot Jesus wants us?

Three statements can direct our calling and service to the Lord and our communities.

- I can't.
- You can.
- I'm here.

"I can't." We are capable of doing many things when we put our minds to them. But nothing we can do on our own will bring peace and fulfillment. When we come to the place of humility, we realize that the work we are called to do is not to boast about us but about Him.

John the Baptist said, "He must become greater; I must become less" (John 3:30). We are to point to and glorify the Messiah, just as John the Baptist did. Submission to the Lord shows our contentment with and gratitude for our role in God's greater plan. Acknowledging our inability to do things without Him is proof of our transformation and commitment to change.

I had a massive problem with submission when I was a young believer. I thought it meant being kicked while I was down. But that isn't the way the Lord sees submission. Accepting and yielding to His superior authority and sovereignty indicates that we understand His wisdom and are ready to implement it in our lives. That takes work.

We execute our responsibility by humbling ourselves, giving over our control to the One who controls all. Once we fall to our knees and confess our inability in comparison to the power of Christ, we begin to allow His supremacy to rule us. We submit to His best for our lives, calling, and purpose. That's true success. We can't, but we know the One who can.

"You can." God can do all things. "Jesus looked at [the disciples] and said, 'With man this is impossible, but with God all things are possible'" (Matthew 19:26).

Jesus works all things for our good as believers. If we stay the course where we are, moving forward, we allow the Holy Spirit's power to do God's work. We can because God has already paid the price. The work He came to do was completed on the cross. Once we submit and accept that He has qualified us to be His tool to fulfill His plan on earth, the submission to His sovereignty supercharges our gifts. Continuing to surrender to God's authority and power keeps us focused on our Holy responsibility to work for the Lord.

"I'm here." The third statement gives God permission to use us. God is a gentleman. He will not force us to fulfill His plan and purpose. He patiently waits for us to give ourselves to Him, to invite the Holy Spirit to move in our lives and pour out to others. Giving ourselves to the Lord's work takes commitment: wherever He takes us to do whatever He asks. It's scary, but not so terrifying when we know the Lord is sovereign.

The prophet Isaiah was frightened when he first saw the glory of the Lord in the temple, but he stepped forward in faith anyway. "Then I heard the voice of the Lord saying, 'Whom shall I send? And who will go for us?' And I said, 'Here am I. Send me!'" (Isaiah 6:8).

Devote your heart to Jesus entirely. God's truth will renew your mind and your soul will yearn to become more like Him. You will fall more in love with Jesus.

Our personal relationship with an almighty God continually reveals our purpose in His plan. We work as if we're working for Him, not our selfish intent. Fulfill His best.

Where will God send us? Exactly where He needs us. Be ready. Say yes before you know where you're going.

Put your faith in play. One day at a time. One person's story.

Transformation. Healing. Work with all your heart.

Leave His fingerprints. Have fun serving Him.

The gospel frees us to take risks and not to worry as we do. We know we can't, but God can and will use us for His glory. Fulfilling God's call brings freedom, joy, and peace of mind.

Detox Challenge

- Begin with prayer.
- Clothe yourself with compassion, kindness, humility, gentleness, patience, forgiveness, and gratitude.
- What is one thing you can begin to do to clothe yourself in each of these virtues?
- Are you ready to take your intentional walk?
  - Confess to the Lord each day:
    - I can't.
    - You can.
    - I'm here.
- Be ready to serve Him with whatever He asks, whenever He calls you to it.

Acknowledgments

Writing a book was more challenging than I imagined and more rewarding than I could expect. Tackling the second book was intimidating. I couldn't have accomplished the second book without the amazing support of my husband, David Jauss. With God, we can achieve more for the kingdom than whatever we plan. I love doing life with you, side by side. I am eternally grateful for you.

To my boys—D. J., Charley, and Will. Thank you for the incredible support. You all have challenged me to be a better person without compromising. I love watching you become the men God created you to be.

Mama, thank you for urging me on and asking me every week when my next book was coming. That put a fire under me!

To my North Carolina family, life has thrown us many curveballs. We can only continue one day at a time. I'm thankful we are doing life together.

Without the experiences and support of the ladies in my baseball family, this book would be boring. You were the first to believe it could be a book. My love for you pushed me through.

A very special thanks to Kathi Lipp for encouraging me to keep writing. Your validation was transformational for me in a time of significant discouragement.

My ladies at Writing at the Red House, you will forever be cherished friends. Wendy, Jenn, Mel, Jennifer, Jan, Kendra, Cheri, Kathi, Kathleen, and Tonya. Together we will help others with our words.

Alice Crider, thank you for validating my belief that this book is needed. Your guidance was invaluable.

Gail Mills, as always, my friend, you are a writing angel. You read it before anyone else and challenged me to be better. Again, I couldn't do a book without you.

Iron Stream, John Herring, and all who had a hand in getting this book on the shelves. Thank you for another chance to impact the kingdom.

Cindy Sproles, my editor, you've challenged me to rise above my elementary grammar and repetitive lists to make this book the very best it could be. Thank you for cheering me on through the process. You are the BEST!

To Denise Loock and Susan Cornell, this book is better because of your meticulous guidance. Thank you!

A very special thank you to my teacher, mentor, and life counselor, Gloria Lyndaker. Without you in my life, I wouldn't be a college graduate or be sane. Your loving guidance has been a lifesaver in many seasons. Forever, my friend.

Jesus, I'm glad I'll never know what life would have been without you. You knew I'd write. I did not.

About the Author

Billie Jauss encourages women to live life on purpose while navigating the obstacles along the way. Known for her passion for inspiring women in their spiritual growth, Billie provides practical and useful biblical guidance for Christian women to find peace and fulfillment.

She's the author of *Making Room: Doing Less So God Can Do More*. Billie is also a speaker with Compassion International. Her podcast, *start small BELIEVE BIG*, offers guidance to live life with meaning, one step, decision, and action at a time.

She has been married to Dave, a Major League Baseball coach, for over thirty years. While raising their three sons, they lived in fifteen cities and towns in the US, Venezuela, and the Dominican Republic. Together they serve Compassion International through child sponsorship and survival programs in the Dominican Republic.